Y0-CCP-202

do-it-yourself do-it-yourself
do-it-yourself do-it-yourself
do-it-yourself do-it-yourself
do-it-you
do-it-you
do-it-you
do-it-you
do-it-yourself do-it-yourself
do-it-yourself do-it-yourself
do-it-yourself do-it-yourself
do-it-yourself do-it-yourself
do-it-yourself do-it-yourself
do-it-yourself do-it-yourself
do-it-yourself do-it-yourself
do-it-yourself do-it-yourself
do-it-yourself do-it-yourself
do-it-yourself do-it-yourself
do-it-yourself do-it-yourself
do-it-yourself do-it-yourself
do-it-yourself do-it-yourself
do-it-yourself do-it-yourself
do-it-yourself do-it-yourself
do-it-yourself do-it-yourself
do-it-yourself do-it-yourself
do-it-yourself do-it-yourself
do-it-yourself do-it-yourself
do-it-yourself do-it-yourself
do-it-yourself do-it-yourself
do-it-yourself do-it-yourself
do-it-yourself do-it-yourself
do-it-yourself do-it-yourself
do-it-yourself do-it-yourself
do-it-yourself do-it-yourself
do-it-yourself do-it-yourself
do-it-yourself do-it-yourself
do-it-yourself do-it-yourself
do-it-yourself do-it-yourself
do-it-yourself do-it-yourself
do-it-yourself do-it-yourself
do-it-yourself do-it-yourself
do-it-yourself do-it-yourself
do-it-yourself do-it-yourself
do-it-yourself do-it-yourself
do-it-yourself do-it-yourself
do-it-yourself do-it-yourself
do-it-yourself do-it-yourself
do-it-yourself do-it-yourself
do-it-yourself do-it-yourself
do-it-yourself do-it-yourself
do-it-yourself do-it-yourself
do-it-yourself do-it-yourself
do-it-yourself do-it-yourself
do-it-yourself do-it-yourself
do-it-yourself do-it-yourself
do-it-yourself do-it-yourself

EXTERIOR
HOME REPAIRS

do-it-yourself do-it-yourself
do-it-yourself do-it-yourself
do-it-yourself do-it-yourself
do-it-yourself do-it-yourself
do-it-yourself do-it-yourself
do-it-yourself do-it-yourself
do-it-yourself do-it-yourself
do-it-yourself do-it-yourself
do-it-yourself do-it-yourself
do-it-yourself do-it-yourself
do-it-yourself do-it-yourself
do-it-yourself do-it-yourself
do-it-yourself do-it-yourself
do-it-yourself do-it-yourself
do-it-yourself do-it-yourself
do-it-yourself do-it-yourself
do-it-yourself do-it-yourself
do-it-yourself do-it-yourself
do-it-yourself do-it-yourself
do-it-yourself do-it-yourself
do-it-yourself do-it-yourself
do-it-yourself do-it-yourself
do-it-yourself do-it-yourself
do-it-yourself do-it-yourself
do-it-yourself do-it-yourself
do-it-yourself do-it-yourself
do-it-yourself do-it-yourself
do-it-yourself do-it-yourself
do-it-yourself do-it-yourself
do-it-yourself do-it-yourself
do-it-yourself do-it-yourself
do-it-yourself do-it-yourself
do-it-yourself do-it-yourself
do-it-yourself do-it-yourself
do-it-yourself do-it-yourself
do-it-yourself do-it-yourself
do-it-yourself do-it-yourself
do-it-yourself do-it-yourself

Editor-in Chief and Series Coordinator
DONALD D. WOLF

Design, Layout and Production
MARGOT L. WOLF

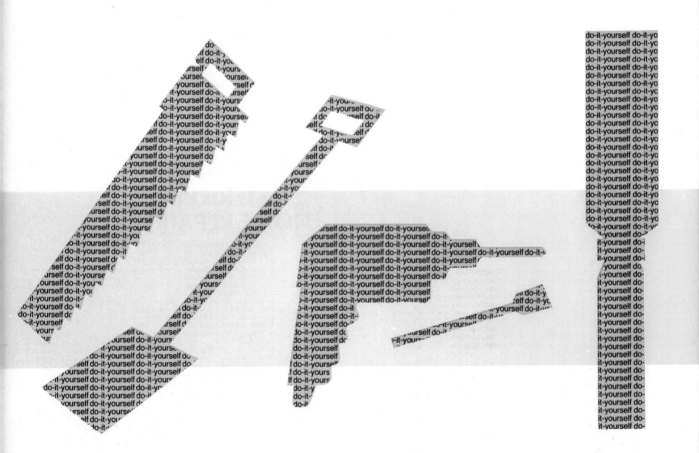

ADVENTURES IN HOME REPAIR SERIES

EXTERIOR HOME REPAIRS

Written by
DICK DEMSKE

Illustrated by
JAMES E. BARRY

Consolidated Book Publishers

NEW YORK • CHICAGO

Introduction

There is pride in home ownership, but there is also work. When you live in an apartment, you leave the care of the outside of the building to someone else. But when you sign up for that mortgage, the burden shifts to you. How heavy that burden is depends on your pocketbook, your attitudes, and your do-it-yourself skills.

Sure, if you can afford it, you can leave everything to somebody else—if you can find such a somebody else. The all-around handyman is a vanishing breed. And it is economically prohibitive to hire a concrete contractor to repair a hairline crack in the driveway or a high-priced carpenter to renail a loose shingle. But those are the little things that must be fixed before they become big things. You can adopt an attitude of letting such problems slide, but you are asking for big headaches in the near future, and besides, what about your pride of possession?

So that brings us to do-it-yourself skills. True, there are some persons who simply can't drive a nail without smashing a thumb. But most of us are blessed with at least basic dexterity, and most exterior repairs do not call for more than that plus common sense. To help you know which jobs fall within your range of skills, we have devised a rating system, based on consultations with professionals in the various building trades, materials manufacturers, and ordinary do-it-yourselfers—like yourself. Projects rated simple enough for just about any homeowner to tackle are designated ● . Those somewhat more difficult, requiring some special skills or knowledge or a bit more experience, are designated ▲ . Those few marked ▮ should be attempted by only the most advanced do-it-yourselfer, or otherwise left to the professionals.

Every effort has been made to ensure the accuracy, reliability, and up-to-dateness of the information and instructions in this book. We are not infallible, however—and neither are you. We cannot guarantee that there are no human or typographical errors herein, nor can we guarantee that you will not err in following our directions. We only hope that, if this happens, it will not lessen the feeling of satisfaction you receive from doing-it-yourself.

DONALD D. WOLF

Copyright © 1978 by
Consolidated Book Publishers
420 Lexington Avenue
New York, New York 10017

All rights reserved under the International
and Pan-American Copyright Conventions.
Manufactured in the United States of America
and published simultaneously in Canada by
George J. McLeod Limited, Toronto, Ontario.

Library of Congress Catalog Card Number: 76-52268
International Standard Book Number: 0-8326-2216-8

Contents

1

The Toolbox

MOST OF THE tools you'll need for working on your home's exterior are the basics with which you are probably familiar. You may already have some or all of them. But if all you have in your toolbox are a cheap hammer and screwdriver, be prepared to accumulate a few more instruments—and good ones, this time.

When you inhabit a furnished room or an apartment, your tool needs are few. But when you (and the bank) own your home, you will find that you need a small arsenal of basic tools to take care of the place. You should start picking up some of them as soon as you sign on the dotted line, watching for bargains and sales (not cheap models, but markdowns of good ones).

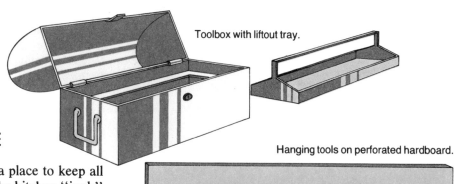

Toolbox with liftout tray.

TOOL STORAGE

You're going to need a place to keep all those shiny new tools. The kitchen "junk" drawer might be okay to start with, but you'll soon find that the screwdriver is hopelessly entangled with string when you want it most. One of the first things you should do in your new home is to make some sort of plan for tool storage. It may be only a toolbox—at first, anyway—but it should be separate, so that you know where the tools are when you need them quickly.

●A good start toward tool storage is a piece of perforated hardboard (popularly

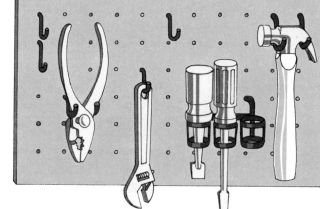

Hanging tools on perforated hardboard.

known as Pegboard, a trade name). When you buy the board, get one of the kits that contain hardware for attaching it to the wall, as well as the hooks, hangers, and assorted accessories for accommodating various tools. Hang it in the basement or garage. Later on, you'll probably want a workbench, so make sure there is room for one underneath your storage wall.

BUYING TOOLS

Does a devoted fisherman buy a cheap rod and reel? Does a dentist buy a bargain-basement drill? Of course not. The same attitude should apply to any tool. The dollar you save on a supermarket or drugstore tool can cost you many times that in time and trouble, so don't buy it. Cheap tools also often chip, break, or collapse, causing expensive damage and even injury.

Always buy quality merchandise. A good hammer is precisely tooled, properly weighted, and has maximum strength so that it will drive a nail straight, true, and fast. A cheap hammer will slip off the nail, drive it crookedly, and require more strokes. Often, the head is poorly attached so that it might fly off at a crucial time and possibly even become a lethal missile. It just isn't worth it. The same applies to all tools.

When you shop, look for tools that are stamped with the manufacturer's name or symbol. Many reputable manufacturers have generous warranties, some for life! Pick up the tool and simulate its use. Does it have a tough and sturdy feel? Is the metal smooth and polished? Anything that gets rugged duty, such as a wrench or hammerhead, should be drop-forged. If there are moving parts, do they work freely and easily without wiggle or play?

CLAW HAMMER

There are many kinds of hammers: ball peen for metalwork, tack for upholstery, mason's for brickwork, to name just a few. What most laymen mean by a "hammer" is the common claw, or nail, hammer. The claw hammer is the basic hammer for jobs like whacking wood into place, but it is designed primarily for driving in or pulling out nails. The best claw hammer for general use has a 16-ounce head that is firmly attached to a wood handle, either with a solid wedge and/or glue on top, or forged in a single piece with the handle which is then covered with rubber, plastic, or leather for a firm grip. A good one costs about $8.

●To use a hammer correctly, grip it at or near the end of the handle and swing it from your shoulder. You may miss the nail at first, but keep trying (on scrap wood) until you get the "swing" of it. It's well worth the practice. An experienced carpenter can drive in large spikes this way with just a couple of blows.

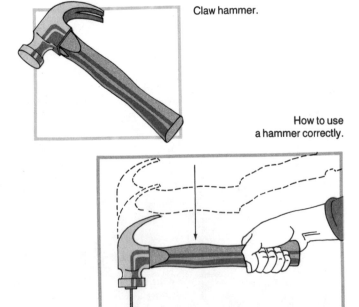

Claw hammer.

How to use a hammer correctly.

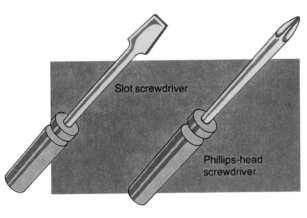

Slot screwdriver.

Phillips-head screwdriver.

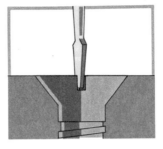

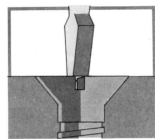

Wrong-size screwdrivers:
Blade too thin for slot (above).

Blade too thick for slot (above right).

Blade too wide for slot (right).

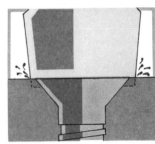

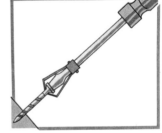

How to make a starter hole with an awl.

Screwdriver with clip to hold screws.

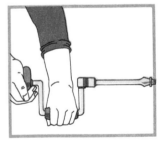

Use two hands on screwdriver.

Screwdriver bit in brace.

SCREWDRIVERS

One screwdriver is not really enough for the do-it-yourselfer's toolbox. To start with, you should have the most common one, with a flat-tipped, wedge-shaped blade ¼ inch wide and about 6 inches long. This model fits the most frequently used sizes of slotted screws, but you shouldn't use it for larger or very tiny sizes. Either the blade will be too small and slip around, or it will be too big and won't fit into the slot. Sometimes the blade will fit the slot but be wider than the screw and damage the surrounding surface. So it's best to have one with a narrow blade. For heavier work, use a screwdriver with a longer shank.

A Phillips screwdriver has an X-shaped end and is used for cross-slotted screws. One of these will do for a start, the most useful being the #2, which has a shank about 4 inches long. Buy others as needed.

A good screwdriver has a tough, tempered-steel blade and a fluted handle, usually plastic. The handle should be smooth and gently rounded at the hand. The tip of the blade is usually polished, but not necessarily the shank.

● A screwdriver is simple to use once the screw is started. Many novices try to use the screwdriver without starting the hole first. This may sometimes work in soft wood but is virtually impossible in hard wood. Use an awl, a nail, or a tool specifically designed for starting screws. Many old-timers start the screw by banging it in with a hammer, but this often results in damaged and hard-to-work screw slots. It is helpful to hold the blade and screw head together in the beginning. This is not always possible, however, and some screwdrivers have metal clips over the blade that hold the screw head to the blade for use in hard-to-reach areas. Firm pressure should be applied against the screw during driving to keep the blade in place. When the wood is very hard, it is wise to predrill the entire hole (use a wood-screw pilot bit; see ELECTRIC DRILL). Special drill bits are available for this purpose, matching screw sizes. It sometimes helps to use both hands once the screw is started, one turning the handle, and the other held flat against the end of it to apply more pressure.

● It is easy to remove screws once you get them loosened. The trouble, again, is getting them started, or "broken." Don't forget that screws are driven in clockwise, and removed counterclockwise. If a screw won't budge, give it a quick twist in both directions. For larger stubborn screws, a screwdriver bit in a brace provides extra leverage.

Quality screwdrivers cost from about $1.50 for small ones to about $4 for large ones. They are often available in sets, which is fine if the set is priced less than the total of the tools inside. Check first, because this isn't always the case.

PLIERS

There are numerous types of pliers, most of them used by specialists such as electricians and electronics workers. The kind the homeowner uses most often is the slip-joint pliers. It performs numerous holding tasks—and is often the wrong tool for the job. Pliers are not really designed for tightening and loosening nuts—wrenches are. Yet this is a common household use, and it will do if you don't have the right wrench in your toolbox.

A slip-joint pliers *is* the right tool for grasping, turning, bending, or pulling bolts, wires, broken glass, and sharp or small objects. The term "slip-joint" is applied because the tool has two slots in which the center fastener pin can be located. In one slot, the pliers grip small objects, with the forward jaws tight and parallel. When the pin is in the other slot, the concave inner jaws can go around larger objects. Some pliers have cutting jaws just inside the curved portion. These are for cutting wires, small nails, etc.

When shopping for pliers, choose ones that have been drop-forged and have either a polished surface or a bluish-black sheen. The pin should be solidly fastened so that you can't remove it. The outer parallel jaws should have fine grooves or cross-hatching, the inner ones sharp, rugged teeth. Handles should be scored or tooled so that you can grip them firmly. A good pair costs about $2 to $3. Special purpose types may be more.

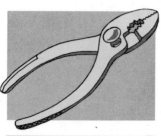
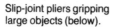

Slip-joint pliers (left).

Slip-joint pliers gripping small objects (below left).

Slip-joint pliers gripping large objects (below).

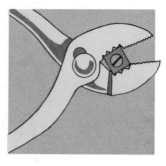

Slip-joint pliers cutting wire.

HANDSAWS

Saws, too, come in a wide variety of sizes and types. The homeowner should purchase an 8- or 10-point crosscut saw for all-around work. The "8-point" means that there are eight teeth per inch. "Crosscut" means that the teeth are beveled slightly outward and knife-shaped, designed for cutting across the grain of the wood—the most common type of cut.

A ripsaw has squarish, chisellike teeth, and it cuts with the grain. Most do-it-yourselfers have little need for a ripsaw. If you must do a lot of ripping, a power saw of some kind is preferred.

A hacksaw is used for cutting metals and some plastics. It has a wide U-shaped frame with devices on each end for holding the removable, fine-toothed saw blade. A thumbscrew draws the blade taut.

A coping saw is somewhat similar in design to a hacksaw, except that the blade is much thinner and has larger teeth. A coping-saw blade can be turned to various angles for making curving cuts in wood.

Keyhole and compass saws are similar, with the keyhole blade being thinner and finer. Both are used to make curving cuts and small cuts when only one side of the work is accessible, such as in paneling, wallboard, and similar materials that are already nailed up.

When buying a saw, look for a tempered steel or chrome-nickel blade. Handles should be removable hardwood or high-

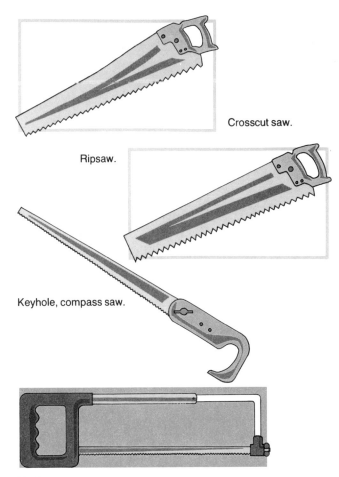

Crosscut saw.

Ripsaw.

Keyhole, compass saw.

Hacksaw.

impact plastic. Better saws have taper-ground blades, and some have a Teflon coating for rust-resistance and less binding.

Crosscut saws—good ones—cost about $10, a hacksaw about half that. Coping saws cost a little less, as do keyhole and compass saws.

MEASURING INSTRUMENTS

A 6-foot folding rule with extension is a good all-around measuring device. The readings are large and easily read, and some have red markings every 16 inches

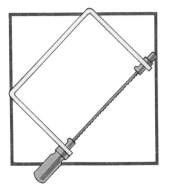

Coping saw.

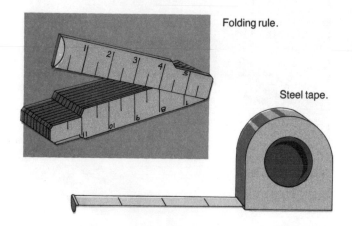

Folding rule.

Steel tape.

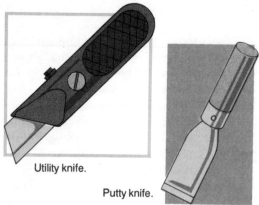

Utility knife.

Putty knife.

(the standard "centering" for framing). The extension is an extra 5-inch section that slides out and allows you to take inside measurements when working in closets, cabinets, etc.

A steel tape is flexible enough to wind up inside a small case, yet rigid enough when extended to stay in place. A small hook on the end holds it in place when you are measuring a long piece. The case usually is exactly 2 or 3 inches long, so that you can measure inside dimensions accurately by adding on the 2 or 3 inches. Some have friction locks to hold the tape open and spring returns to retract it quickly.

A good folding rule with extension costs about $5; a steel tape ½ inch wide by 10 feet costs a dollar or so less.

UTILITY KNIFE

This is an inexpensive tool that has a multitude of uses. It utilizes a razor blade, or a special blade that looks like one, to cut such things as gypsum wallboard, wallcoverings, thin woods, carpeting, rope, and string. It is also handy for opening boxes and cartons.

A good utility knife has a handle shaped to fit your palm, with space inside to store extra blades. Look for one that has a re-

tractable blade that you can withdraw for safety's sake when not in use. The retracting device also lets you extend it to various lengths to adjust for the thickness of whatever you are cutting. The knife costs about $2 to $3.

PUTTY KNIFE

This tool is used for applying and smoothing soft materials such as putty and wood filler. Those with stiffer blades can also be used as scrapers.

A good putty knife has a blade that extends well into the handle and is attached by rivets. The blade should be of hardened, tempered steel with a blunt end and no sharp edges. You will pay about $1.50 for a 1½-inch-wide putty knife, and up to $3 for a 3-inch model.

CHISELS

A wood chisel consists of a steel blade usually fitted with a wooden or plastic handle. It has a single beveled cutting edge on the end of the blade. According to construction, chisels are divided into two general classes: tang chisels, in which part of the chisel enters the handle, and socket

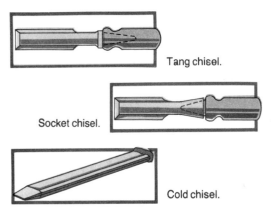

Tang chisel.

Socket chisel.

Cold chisel.

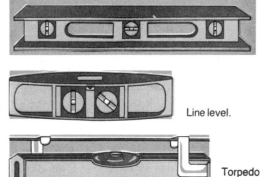

Carpenter's level.

Line level.

Torpedo level.

chisels, in which the handle enters into a part of the chisel. A socket chisel is designed for striking with a wooden mallet (never a steel hammer), whereas a tang chisel is designed for hand use only.

Wood chisels are also divided into types, depending upon their weight and thickness, the shape or design of the blade, and the work they are intended to do. For general household use, a ½-inch or ¾-inch paring chisel is probably best. It has a relatively thin blade and is beveled along the sides. The cost is $3 to $4.

Another type of chisel for your exterior-repair toolbox is the cold chisel. This is made of hardened, tempered alloy steel and is used for striking steel, concrete, stone, and other hard materials. A cold chisel is struck with a ball peen or other heavy hammer. It costs a little less than a wood chisel of the same size.

LEVELS

The carpenter's level is a tool designed to determine whether a plane or surface is true horizontal or true vertical. It is a simple instrument consisting of a liquid, such as alcohol or chloroform, partially filling a glass vial or tube so that a bubble remains. The vial is mounted in a frame of alumi-

num, magnesium, or wood. Levels are usually equipped with two or more vials. One vial is built into the frame at right angles to another. The vial is slightly curved, causing the bubble always to seek the highest point in the tube. On the outside of the vial are two sets of gradation lines separated by a space. Leveling is established when the air bubble is centered between the gradation lines.

There are several other types of levels. A torpedo level is useful in tight places. It has a top-reading vial so that you can place it on a low or deep surface and tell whether it's level without bending way down to look at it. A line level hooks onto a piece of twine or string and is useful when working with concrete forms, brick, and similar jobs where lines are used.

WRENCHES

There are probably more types of wrenches than of any other tool. There are open-end and box wrenches, some with a combination of each, and some with half-boxes. (A box wrench completely encloses the nut.) There are ratchet wrenches that are turned like a crank, pipe wrenches, chain wrenches, and countless others.

Your first wrench acquisition should be

Adjustable wrench.

an adjustable wrench. These come in various sizes, but one about 8 inches long, with jaw capacity up to an inch, is a good starter. This wrench has one fixed jaw, and another that is moved away from or toward the fixed jaw by means of a knurled knob.

Look for a drop-forged, alloy steel wrench with a chrome-polished or blue-black sheen. The jaws should be exactly parallel and not loose (check that by wiggling the movable jaw). Some have a locking device that holds the adjustable jaw in a constant position. A quality adjustable wrench of the recommended size costs about $5.

ELECTRIC DRILL

An electric drill can do so many jobs that it is almost a must in the do-it-yourselfer's toolbox. With it you can make holes in almost any material. By using accessories and attachments you can sand, polish, grind, buff, stir paint, and drive screws.

Depending on quality, size, gearing, and special features, a drill for home use costs from $10 to $50 or more. Your best choice will be a model with the work capacity and special features you will regularly use. The work capacity of a drill depends on its chuck size and rated revolutions per minute (RPM).

The chuck size is the diameter of the largest bit shank the drill chuck can hold. Home-use sizes are ¼, ⅜, and ½ inch. Usually, the larger the chuck, the wider and deeper the holes the drill can bore.

The RPM rating is an indication of the number of gear sets in a model, its speed, and the type of work for which it is best suited. For example, a ¼-inch drill rated about 2,000 RPM usually has one gear set and is appropriate for rapid drilling in wood and use with sanding and polishing accessories. A model with more gears would have a

lower RPM rating and work more slowly but could make bigger holes in hard metals or masonry without stalling or overheating.

For most jobs around a home, a single-speed drill is adequate. However, a two-speed or variable-speed model would be more suitable if you intend to drill material (such as glass) that requires a slow speed or if you want to use many accessories. A drill with both variable speed and reverse is effective for driving and removing screws.

The trigger switch, which starts the drill, is on the pistol-grip handle, and many models include a switch lock for continuous operation. You activate the lock by pressing a button; the lock instantly releases if you tighten your squeeze on the trigger switch.

Variable-speed drills have trigger switches that allow you to vary bit speed from almost zero up to maximum RPM by trigger-finger pressure. Some have controls for presetting the maximum RPM.

Drills with reverse have separate reverse controls in different positions depending on the brand. To protect the motor, allow the drill to come to a full stop before reversing.

The front of the drill, where bits and other accessories are inserted and removed, is called the chuck. The three-jaw gear type is the most common. Its collar is first hand-closed on the shank of a bit. Then a key is inserted into the chuck body and turned to tighten the three jaws simultaneously and with considerable force. Some models have a holder to make key loss less likely.

Some bargain drills have chucks that are hand-tightened by means of knurled collars. They may either offer a poor hold on bits and accessories or be difficult to loosen when work is finished. Examine chuck placement as well as quality. The higher the chuck on the front of the housing, the easier the drill will be to use in corners.

Manufacturers' catalogs contain information on the accessories available for particular drill brands and models. The com-

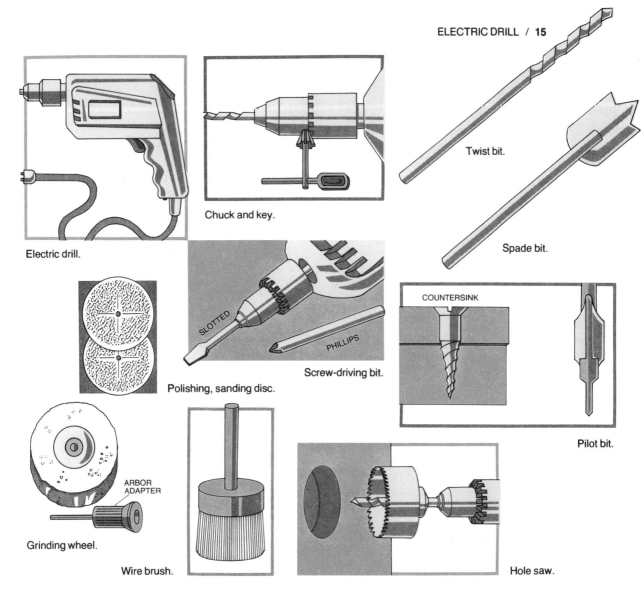

Electric drill.

Chuck and key.

Twist bit.

Spade bit.

SLOTTED

PHILLIPS

Screw-driving bit.

COUNTERSINK

Polishing, sanding disc.

Pilot bit.

ARBOR
ADAPTER

Grinding wheel.

Wire brush.

Hole saw.

mon accessories that enable you to use a drill for various jobs are described here.

A drill bit has a working end that makes holes and a smooth shank that is grasped by the jaws of a chuck. Although bits can be bought individually, they cost less if purchased in sets.

The twist bit, the most commonly used, cuts cylindrical holes. It has a sharp point and two spiral-shaped cutting edges that lift chips out of the hole as the bit turns. Carbon steel twist bits are suited to drilling wood and soft metals; high-speed steel bits cut wood, soft metals, and mild steel; tungsten carbide or carbide-tipped bits cut hard metals and masonry. Cutting diameters commonly available range from $1/16$ inch to $1/2$ inch.

The spade bit cuts large cylindrical holes in wood. It has a flat, spade-shaped driving end with a pointed tip. Common cutting diameters range from $3/8$ inch to 1 inch.

The wood-screw pilot bit has three widths of cutting edge. The narrowest drills a hole to give screw threads solid anchorage. The next makes a shaft for the unthreaded screw shank. The widest makes a hole, or countersink, for flat-headed screws. A detachable stop can make shallow or deep countersinks.

The screw-driving bit attaches to drills

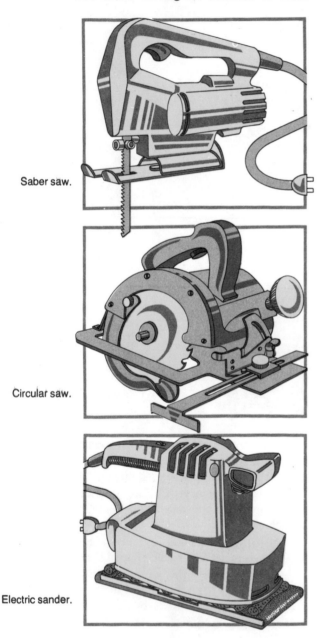

Saber saw.

Circular saw.

Electric sander.

with variable speed and reverse to drive and remove slotted and Phillips-head screws. On single- or two-speed drills, the bit must be used with a special screw-driving attachment.

Polishing and sanding discs, grinding wheels, wire-brush discs, and hole saws are usually secured to a drill by an arbor that goes through the center hole of the wheel or disc and is fastened by a washer and nut or by a screw and washer. A flange keeps the wheel from slipping down the shank that fits into the drill chuck. Some discs and wire brushes have built-in shanks that fit the drill spindle when the chuck is removed.

Discs are used either with abrasive paper for sanding or a soft bonnet for polishing. Grinding wheels are for sharpening tools or smoothing metal. Wire brushes remove paint, rust, and dirt from wood and metal. Hole saws cut round holes through boards or sheet materials by means of a rim saw blade and a centered pilot bit. Common diameters range from ½ inch to 4 inches.

OTHER TOOLS

There are literally hundreds of specialized tools that you may use for specific tasks. Buy these as the need arises, as your skills increase, and as you undertake more detailed work around the house—especially if you begin making improvements as well as routine repairs. Power tools will make your work easier and the results better. The ones you will probably buy are: a saber saw, for fast cutting of curved and straight lines in wood and other materials; a circular saw, for extensive cutting of straight lines and invaluable for major jobs such as installing wood siding; and an electric sander, for smooth, speedy removal of wood, paint, or anything else removable by regular sandpaper.

2

Roofs, Gutters, Downspouts

MODERN ROOFING technology is the product of centuries of trial-and-error experimentation combined with up-to-date knowledge of roofing materials. Properly installed, today's roofs will provide years and years of virtually maintenance-free service.

Occasionally, however (especially in harsher climates), roofing materials may fall victim to the elements. Continuous exposure to intense sunlight may cause cracking in asphalt shingles. Improper drainage can result in faulty roof performance.

Thus, the choice of style and composition of roofs often depends on climatic conditions. In some tropical countries, for example, palm leaves make a perfectly adequate house roof.

In North America, where the weather ranges from tropical to arctic, many types of roofing are used. Most of the United States and Canada, however, lie in the temperate zone, and roofs are very similar in all but the extreme hot and cold zones of these countries. In practical terms, this means that most roofs are of peaked wood trusses, or rafters, covered by either plywood or wood sheathing and finished with a layer of mineral-surfaced asphalt shingles. There are other types, of course, wood shingles, slate, tile, and asbestos-cement being fairly common. Other materials such as metal, metal-bound gypsum, reinforced concrete, or concrete planks are sometimes used—mostly on flat roofs.

Roofings of various types may be and frequently are applied over old roofs, but it is usually advisable to remove the old roofing before applying an entirely new roof—particularly if one new roof has already been applied over the original. The homeowner then has the opportunity to have defective or rotted sheathing replaced, thus providing a smoother roof deck with opportunity for better nailing.

Sometimes the do-it-yourselfer prefers to leave roofing repairs to the professional. Unless the roof is low or flat, there is certainly some danger in climbing around on it. Even so, it pays to know something about roofing—if only to keep an eye on the roofer and his bill.

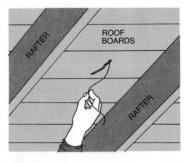

1. Locate hole from beneath and mark with wire (left).

2. Coat leak with asphalt (below left).

3. Nail board beneath leak (below).

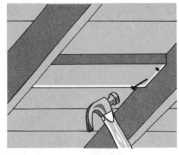

MAKING REPAIRS

When a leak develops, it is important that repairs be made without unnecessary delay. If repairs are neglected over a long period, interior plaster may crack, loosen, and eventually fall. Drywall becomes soggy and crumbly, and the whole roof structure below the shingling may rot. Even small leaks often cause discoloration of wall coverings and stains on finished floors. Although it may not be possible to apply a new roof or to do extensive repair work, the do-it-yourselfer may be able to patch leaky spots until permanent repairs can be made or the old roof can be replaced.

It is often difficult to locate the point of leakage from a wet spot on the ceiling, especially if the underside of the roof is not easily accessible, because water may flow along the roof boards or rafters before dripping down. It is equally difficult to locate a hole from the top of the roof. If the attic has no ceiling, however, most holes may be found readily from the inside of the attic on a bright day. Even small holes will be plainly visible, and their location can be marked by pushing wires through to the surface.

You can make a temporary repair from underneath to hold until you can do the job properly from above. Coat the leaking area with asphalt roofing cement. Cut a 1 x 6 or similar board to fit between the rafters, and toenail it in place beneath the asphalt patch.

When making repairs on the roof, wear sneakers or rubber-soled work shoes. Avoid unnecessary walking on the roof, as this can damage the surface.

Make sure your ladder is sound before using it. Place the ladder flat on the ground and walk along the rungs from one end to the other to make sure they are all solid. Check the hooks on an extension ladder to make sure they engage fully.

To raise a long ladder, set its foot against

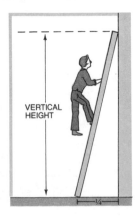

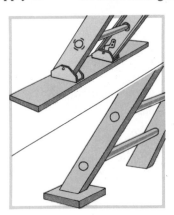

Place ladder against wall, "walk" upright. (far left).

Move foot of ladder out one-quarter of height. (center).

Use boards to level if necessary (left).

Chapter 2 ● Roofs, Gutters, Downspouts

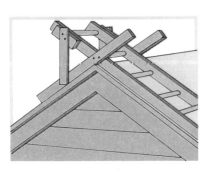

Nail braces to end of ladder and hook over roof ridge (far left).

Ladder held by rope (left).

a wall. Starting at the opposite end, lift it over your head and walk it, rung by rung, until it is upright. Then move the foot away from the wall one-quarter of the height the ladder is to reach. Make sure that the ladder rests on a firm footing. If necessary, place it on a secure board or boards to make the footing level.

Don't attempt to work on a steep roof without some additional support. One way to provide this is with a second ladder (not the one you use to get up to the roof). Nail or screw a piece of 2 x 4 to each leg of the ladder, following the angle of the roof. Nail or screw braces of 1-inch lumber or ¾-inch plywood across the joint (you will have to back these up with blocks of 2 x 4 affixed firmly to the ladder legs). Then "hook" the braced end of the ladder over the peak of the roof.

Another means of support is a strong rope tied to a ladder. Of course it must be firmly anchored or it will be worse than worthless. Tie one end to the top of a flat ladder laid across the roof and secure the other end to a stout tree or other support.

ASPHALT ROOFING

Asphalt-prepared roofings are manufactured in three forms: mineral-surfaced shingles, mineral-surfaced roll roofing, and smooth-surfaced roll roofing. Mineral-surfaced asphalt shingles and roll roofings are composed of roofing felt, made of organic fibers saturated and coated on both sides with asphalt, then surfaced with mineral granules on the side exposed to the weather. The other side may be dusted with mica or talc. Smooth-faced roll roofing is dusted on both sides with fine mineral matter such as mica, talc, or fine sand and is usually lighter in weight than mineral-surfaced roll roofing. Mineral-surfaced asphalt shingles and roll roofing are usually available in a variety of colors; smooth-surfaced roll roofing is usually black or gray.

Mineral-surfaced asphalt shingles are made in strips of two to four (usually three) units or tabs joined together, as well as in the form of individual shingles. When laid, strip shingles furnish virtually the same pattern as individual shingles, and they have become the standard method of application today. Most shingles come in varying sizes and patterns.

The principal cause of damage to asphalt shingle roofs is the action of strong winds

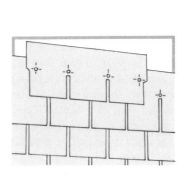
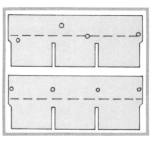

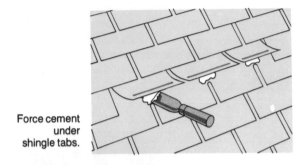

Force cement under shingle tabs.

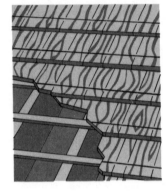

Mark wood shingles for nailing surfaces.

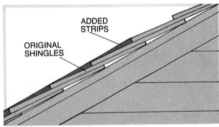

ADDED STRIPS

ORIGINAL SHINGLES

Nail beveled strips for uniform surface at the base of the old shingle.

on shingles that have been nailed too close to the upper edges. Most shingles today are impregnated on the edges with a material that softens in the sun and seals the edges to the shingles below.

The shingles most likely to be affected by winds are those in the four to five courses near the ridge or in the area extending about 5 feet from the sloping area at the edge or rake of the roof. To fasten loose shingles correctly, use a putty knife or trowel to place a small quantity of asphalt cement under the center of each tab about

one inch from the lower edge. Press the shingle down firmly after application. Too much cement will prevent the tab from lying flat. Also, be careful not to seal the lower edge completely.

Asphalt shingles are frequently applied over old wood shingles or other roofing, provided that the surface of the old covering is in reasonably good condition. If not, the old covering should be removed. A wood shingle roof is laid over intermittent wood strips, so be sure to mark the location of the strips to make sure that the new nails will strike a solid surface below. All defective or missing shingles should be replaced, and beveled strips ⅜ inch x 4 inches (the same thickness as the old wood shingles) should be nailed at the base of the old shingles to assure a uniform surface.

If the old covering is completely removed, the roof deck should be made smooth and solid, and all loose material should be swept off. Any defects in the sheathing or plywood should be corrected, and, if the old material is in very bad shape, the entire surface should be recovered with exterior plywood to form a solid new underlayment.

Mineral-surfaced roll roofings are made in various colors, both solid and blended. The mineral granules on the surface protect the asphalt coatings from the weather and increase the fire-resistant qualities of the roofing. The manufacturer's directions should be followed with respect to storing, handling, and temperatures at which roll roofing should be laid.

Minor damage to mineral-surfaced roll roofing such as nail holes or small breaks may be repaired by applying asphalt cement. To repair large breaks, the horizontal seam below the break should be opened and a strip of roofing of the type originally used slipped in under the break, allowing the strip to extend at least 6 inches beyond the break on either side. The lower edge

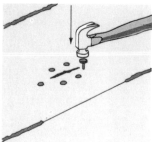

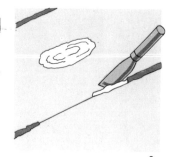

To repair large breaks:

1. Raise seam, slip
   in strip of roofing.
2. Nail around break.
3. Reseal seam.

1   2   3

should be flush with the horizontal exposed edge. Asphalt cement should be applied liberally on the upper surface of the repair strip before inserting it. After the strip has been inserted, press the edges of the roofing down firmly and nail securely with rustproof nails. Space the nails 2 inches apart about ¾ inch from the edge of the break. Apply asphalt cement to the horizontal seam and renail; cement over nails.

Leaks at the seams of roll roofing are caused principally by inadequate nailing and cementing of the roofing, by loose nails, and by buckling of the roofing at the seams. To repair leaky seams, sweep out the seams to remove accumulated dust and dirt, cut all buckles that terminate at the seams, and insert a strip of roofing in the same manner as for larger breaks.

▲Roll roofing may be applied over old wood shingles or other roofing materials, providing that the surface of the old covering is in reasonably good condition and that it has been made smooth in the same manner as for mineral-surfaced asphalt shingles. Otherwise, the worn roofing should be removed and the roof deck prepared in the same manner as for the application of asphalt shingles. Follow the directions supplied by the manufacturer.

Although smooth-surfaced roll roofings were fairly common at one time, their use for surfacing is not recommended today. Asphalt shingles are the preferred treatment, and mineral-covered roll roofing is a less expensive second choice. Smooth-surfaced asphalt does not weather as well because the coatings are not protected from the action of sunlight by mineral granules. If you already have such a roof, however, you should know how to maintain it. Also, these roofings can be used for outbuildings and temporary structures at a lower cost than the others. Maintenance instructions, plus application materials, usually come with each package of roll roofing.

To achieve the best service, this roofing material should be recoated at regular intervals with bituminous roof coating. Seams that have opened should be recemented and any small holes in the covering filled with asphalt cement. Loose nails should be pulled, the resulting holes sealed with asphalt cement, and new nails driven.

Coating materials are usually composed of an asphaltic base and mineral fiber, thinned to heavy brushing consistency with

Cut buckled areas of
roll roofing.

Pull loose nail, fill hole
before recoating.

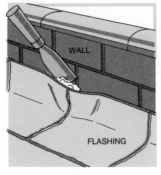
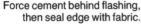

Force cement behind flashing, then seal edge with fabric.

Prepare break in flashing with saturated flashing felt.

a volatile solvent. Fatty acid pitch-base coatings are also available. Follow the directions of the manufacturer.

Smooth-surfaced roll roofing may be applied over other roofing, provided that the surface of the old covering is not too badly deteriorated. When this type of roofing has to be removed, it is suggested in most cases that mineral-coated roofing be applied for longer, less maintenance-prone wear.

BUILT-UP ROOFINGS

The application of built-up roofing is a specialized operation that requires particular experience and special equipment. It is therefore advisable to employ an experienced roofing concern to lay or repair this type of roofing.

Built-up roofing is used when the roof is flat or has a very low pitch. It consists of several layers of bituminous-impregnated felt, lapped and cemented together with a bitumen that is usually heated. Fine gravel or slag is then spread over the top layer to provide a weathering surface. If properly applied, built-up roofings should not require major repairs for a long time.

When a leak occurs in a built-up roof, flashings at parapet walls, skylights, and vents should be carefully inspected, be-

cause the initial failures usually occur at these locations. Bituminous flashings are made of saturated felt and flashing cement. Flashing cement should be forced behind the felt if it has separated from the wall at the upper edge, and the edge should be sealed with a strip of bituminous-saturated cotton fabric 4 inches wide, embedded in and coated with flashing cement.

A break in the flashing should be repaired by applying saturated flashing felt in pieces extending not less than 6 inches in all directions beyond the break, cementing it to the flashing and coating it with flashing cement. Sheet-metal flashings that have a ferrous-metal base, such as zinc-coated sheet iron, should be painted with corrosion-resistant paint or, if badly weathered, replaced with new flashing.

Bare spots on a built-up roof where the mineral surfacing is not properly embedded should be swept or scraped clean and a heavy coating of hot bitumen applied, and additional gravel or slag should be spread not less than 6 inches beyond the other layers. This is definitely a job for the pros.

SLATE ROOFINGS

Slate is a rigid roof material that gives good service and long life with very little need for repair. Though originally more costly, it is usually worth the extra expense. Slate is dense, nonporous rock used on roofs to produce a good-looking, highly durable covering. Only responsible and experienced slate roofers should be engaged to lay such a roof.

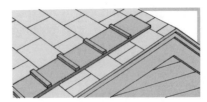

"Chicken ladder."

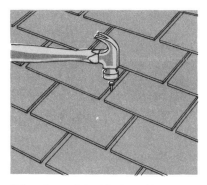

1. Remove broken slates by undercutting the nails.

2. Insert new slate shingle and fasten it, nailing through overlying slate.

3. Insert a piece of sheet copper over the nail head.

The most frequently needed repair of slate roofs is the replacement of broken slates. When such replacement is necessary, supports such as a "chicken ladder" or ladder hooks should be used to distribute the weight of the worker. Broken slates should be removed by undercutting the nails with a hacksaw blade. A new slate shingle of the same color and size as the old one should be inserted and fastened by nailing through the vertical joint of the slates in the overlying course approximately 2 inches below the butt of the slate in the second course above. A piece of sheet copper about 3 x 8 inches should be inserted over the nail head to extend about 2 inches under the second course above the replaced shingle. The metal strip should be bent slightly before being inserted so that it will stay securely in place.

Very old slate roofs sometimes fail because the nails used to fasten the slates have rusted. In such cases, the entire roof covering is removed and replaced, including the felt underlay materials—obviously, a job for a roofer. The sheathing and rafters should be examined and any broken boards replaced with new material. Loose boards should be nailed in place, and before the felt is laid the sheathing should be swept clean, protruding nails driven in, and rough edges trimmed smooth.

Asphalt-saturated felt should then be applied horizontally over the entire roof deck, with the sheets lapped not less than 6 inches and over ridges and hips not less than 12 inches. The sheets should be secured along laps and exposed with large-head roofing nails spaced 6 inches apart.

All slates that are still in good condition may be salvaged and relaid. New slates should be the same size as the old ones and should match them as nearly as possible in color and texture. If an exact match is not possible, alternate the new and old so as not to leave one part old slate and the other new slate with a noticeable difference in shade.

TILE ROOFINGS

The most commonly used roofing tile consists of molded hard-burned shale or mixtures of shale and clay, but metal tile is also available. Good clay tile is hard, fairly dense, and durable and may be obtained in a variety of shapes and textures. Most roofing tile of clay is unglazed, although glazed roofing tile is sometimes used in homes.

Clay tile roofings that have been properly manufactured and applied require very little maintenance. If a tile is broken, it

Remove tile with a nail ripper.

Cement new one in place.

should be removed with a nail ripper and replaced with a new tile of the same color as the original set in roofing cement.

■ Clay tile can be applied over an old roof covering provided that the covering is in reasonably good condition. The roof framing should be examined to determine whether or not the additional weight of the tile can be carried safely and, if not, additional framing or bracing should be added. A competent contractor is best consulted at this stage. Where the old roofing is left in place, all defective portions should be repaired and the surface made as smooth and solid as possible. If the old roof covering is too worn or damaged to provide a proper laying surface for the new tile, it should be removed and the sheathing or roof decking made smooth and solid.

ASBESTOS-CEMENT SHINGLES

Asbestos-cement shingles are manufactured from portland cement (see CHAPTER 7) and asbestos fiber formed in molds under high pressure. The finished product is hard, fairly tough, and durable. Asbestos-cement shingles are available in a variety of colors and textures and may be obtained in rectangular, square, and hexagonal shapes, in single or multiple units.

Asbestos-cement shingles usually require little maintenance. Occasionally, however, a shingle may become broken and need replacement. The broken shingle should be removed by cutting or drawing out the old nails with a ripper (as with slate or tile roofing). A new shingle, similar to the old one, is then inserted. The new shingle should be fastened by nailing through the vertical joint between the shingles in the overlying course approximately 2 inches below the butt-end of the shingle in the second course above. A piece of sheet copper about 3 x 8 inches should be inserted over the nail head and should extend about 2 inches under the course above. The metal should be bent slightly before insertion to hold it firmly in place (see SLATE ROOFINGS earlier in this chapter).

■ Asbestos-cement shingles may be applied over an old roof covering if the roof is in reasonably good condition. The framing should be inspected and, if necessary, reinforced to carry the additional weight of the new shingles safely. If the new roofing is to be laid over old wood shingles, loose shingles should be securely nailed. Warped, split, or decayed shingles should be replaced.

If the old roofing is in poor condition, it may be more economical to remove it entirely than to make the repairs necessary to provide a sound, smooth surface for the new roofing. If the old roofing is removed, loose sheathing boards should be securely nailed and defective material replaced. If

Nail loose sheathing.

the sheathing is in very bad shape, perhaps it would pay to recover the entire surface with exterior plywood.

WOOD SHINGLES

Factors that influence the service life of wood-shingle roofs are pitch and exposure of the roof, durability of the wood in the shingles (red cedar is best), preservative treatment of the shingles, and kind of nails used in fastening.

Wood shingles are usually manufactured in lengths of 16, 18, and 24 inches and in random widths varying from 2½ to 14 inches. On roofs of average pitch, shingles should be laid with about one-fourth of their length exposed. On steeper pitches, the exposure should not exceed one-third the length of the shingle.

On new roofs, wood shingles are frequently laid on open sheathing or slats to permit ventilating the underside. An open deck not only costs less but permits the shingles to dry quickly. The slats are usually 1 x 4-inch boards, spaced to accommodate the nailing of the shingles.

Hot-dipped zinc-coated nails of the proper size and shape are generally recommended for fastening wood shingles, although blued-steel nails may also be used. Longer nails are required for reroofing over old coverings than for new construction.

●Wood shingles that are cracked do not necessarily cause leaks unless the courses are not lined up properly, in which case they may admit moisture to the nail heads in the course below and cause nail failure. To stop the leak, a piece of tin or copper may be placed under the cracked shingle.

Wood shingles may be applied to old roofs as well as new. If the old roofing is in reasonably good condition, it need not be removed. Before applying the new shingles, all warped or deteriorated shingles

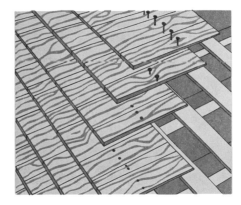

Slats for wood shingles.

1. Place copper beneath cracked shingle.

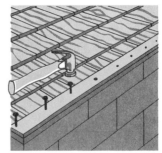

2. Cut off first row of old shingles.

3. Nail 1 x 4 in the space.

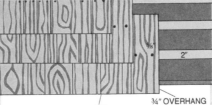
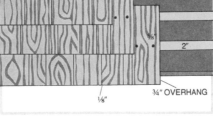

⅜"

2"

¾" OVERHANG

⅛"

4. Space new shingles 1/8-inch apart and nail them down.

5. Use chalk line to keep shingles straight.

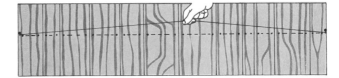

Double shingles at eaves.

should be tightly nailed or replaced. To finish the edges of the roofing, the exposed portion of the first row of old shingles along the eaves should be cut off with a sharp roofer's hatchet or saw, and a 1 x 4 wood strip nailed in the space with the outer edge flush with the eave line. Treat the edges along the gable ends in a similar manner. New shingles should be spaced approximately ⅛ inch apart to allow for expansion in wet weather. They should project between ½ and ¾ inch beyond the edge of the eaves. Each shingle should be fastened with at least two nails placed about ⅝ inch from the edges and about 2 inches under the overlap of the course above; the nails must penetrate the slats to which the original shingles are nailed. The lines of the shingles may be kept parallel to the eaves and ridges by checking the course with a chalk line.

If it becomes necessary to remove the old roofing, the deck should be prepared in the same manner as for a new roof. New shingles should be doubled at the eaves and should project from ½ to ¾ inch beyond the eaves. Courses should be properly aligned and shingles spaced and nailed as above.

ROOF DRAINAGE

Every house, regardless of what type of roofing material is employed, should be equipped with some method of carrying off and effectively dispensing with the large volumes of rainwater that can otherwise create a number of structural problems. Without such a system, water can seep into the earth around the building and cause wet basements, wood decay, peeling paint, and even termite damage. A typical rainfall drainage system includes gutters, downspouts, and leaders to bring the water to the ground and a storm sewer or drywell to absorb the water.

Most gutters today are made from galvanized steel, copper, or aluminum, although wood gutters can still be found on many older structures. In recent years, fiberglass drainage systems have been introduced, and their beneficial features (relatively light weight, ease of installation, etc.) are making them more and more attractive to home builders and renovators.

Metal gutters should be painted to avoid the corrosive, oxidizing actions of the weather. Galvanized gutters may otherwise rust once the thin zinc coating wears away, and unpainted copper gutters will stain adjoining surfaces. A thin coating of roofing cement on the inside of galvanized steel gutters will help prevent rusting.

Wood gutters should be treated with wood preservatives and then coated with exterior paint. Lining the inside of these gutters with roofing cement will further prevent decay. Small holes in wood gutters can

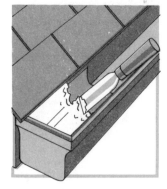

Patch wood gutters with tarpaper and asphalt cement.

be patched with pieces of tarpaper and asphalt cement.

Because water seeks its own level, a slight downward pitch to the drainage end of the gutter is necessary. If there is not enough pitch, the water will not flow effectively to the downspout. A sagging gutter will alter the pitch and, hence, reduce the flow rate. This can cause the gutter to overflow and will hasten rusting and other corrosive actions.

One way to check gutter pitch is to pour a pail of water in the end of the gutter opposite the downspout or leader end. Make note of the areas where water accumulates—it is these areas that need modification. You may need gutter hangers (available at most hardware stores for a small price) to increase the pitch or elevate a sagging length of gutter.

Leaves and other debris can impair the efficiency of a gutter. Periodic cleaning, especially after a storm, will prevent debris from accumulating. To save yourself the time involved with these cleaning operations, you may wish to install wire gutter guards. These work in much the same way that a screen door prevents insects from coming indoors, although here the idea is to prevent leaves from entering the gutters. Downspouts should be equipped with similar screens to strain out the debris and thus prevent clogging.

In the winter months, especially in areas where heavy snowfalls are common, ice and snow may pile up in the gutters instead of harmlessly sliding off the roof. The weight of accumulated snow is often enough to pull gutters loose. To avoid problems of this sort, the outside edges of the gutters should be hung lower than the edge of the roof eaves. This allows ice to slide off without taking the gutter along. If this does not prevent the buildup, it would be wise to install electric heating cables in areas where accumulation is a problem.

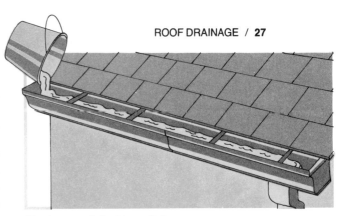

Check gutter pitch with a pail of water.

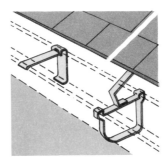

Gutter hanger.

Gutter guard.

Downspout strainer.

Gutters should slant outward.

Electric heating cable for areas where ice and snow accumulation is a problem.

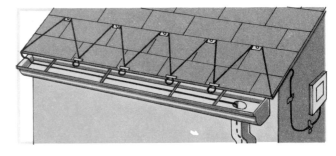

Flush downspout with garden hose once a year.

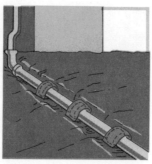

Trench, lined with clay tile, to carry away water.

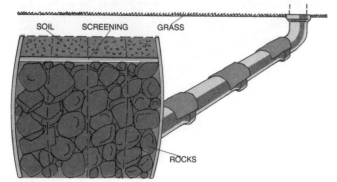

SOIL   SCREENING   GRASS

ROCKS

Simple drywell.

Large drywell.

DOWNSPOUTS

With a good strainer properly installed, downspouts rarely become clogged. Nonetheless, it is a good idea to flush them out once a year with a garden hose, thus forcing out small particles that could accumulate and become a clogging problem.

Many household drainage systems end with the downspout, and the water merely flows into the soil beneath it. This keeps the soil constantly damp and provides an ideal breeding ground for insects, including termites. Wood decay is accelerated by the dampness, and structural damage can occur to concrete foundations. To avoid these often costly problems, the downspout discharge should be carried a safe distance (at least 8 to 10 feet) away from the house.

This can be accomplished by digging a shallow trench of the required length (with a downgrade, of course, away from the downspout). Line the trench with clay tile, covering joints with tarpaper before backfilling. If the soil that the tile empties into is absorbent, no other efforts are required. If not, some alternate means of disposal must be found.

Never connect the drainage system to a septic tank or cesspool that handles your household sewage. Many municipalities allow rainwater runoff to flow into community sewer lines—others forbid this practice because a heavy rainfall may overflow raw sewage at the treatment plant.

If your community does not allow rain drainage into a sewer, a drywell can be constructed to handle the runoff problem. To make a simple drywell, dig a hole big enough to accommodate a large wooden barrel. Remove the top and bottom of the barrel and then place it in the hole. Fill the barrel with rocks up to approximately 5 inches from the top; cover with screening. Fill the remaining space with soil. Lead drainage tiles into the drywell.

For larger houses, or in areas where heavy rainfalls are the norm, bigger drywells may be necessary. These can be built in the same fashion as cesspools—large holes lined with masonry blocks laid without mortar. The tops of the wells should be covered with reinforced concrete set below the ground level.

3

Exterior Walls

PEOPLE COMMONLY refer to "a roof over their heads" as a euphemism for their domiciles, but the roof isn't much good without some solid walls. It didn't take primitive man long to realize that, although trees may afford some shelter from rain, they don't provide much protection against the elements and enemies—so he moved into a cave with solid walls. Today's homeowner or apartment dweller may like to roll back the walls of his "cave" to enjoy a balmy summer night, but they are quickly closed when the winds blow or a storm threatens.

As your home's first line of defense against the elements, the outside walls take quite a beating. They are exposed to extremes of heat and cold and are bombarded by rain, snow, sleet, hail, ice, the harsh rays of the sun, and foul tips off the bats of backyard big leaguers. Small wonder that—whether they be of masonry, wood, or some other material—they occasionally need some attention. Little things like loose mortar joints in brick or splits in clapboard should be repaired before they become major problems, which the ravages of the weather almost guarantee they will.

TAKE A CALK WALK

Any place where two dissimilar materials meet around the house is an open invitation to the invasion of moisture, which will almost surely lead to decay and structural weakness. Calking compound is the material used to seal these joints. It is available in any hardware store, paint supply store, or lumberyard, along with the cartridge-type calking gun. With just a little practice, any do-it-yourselfer can apply the calking in a neat strip.

Calking compound does not completely harden; it forms a tough surface "skin" while remaining soft and flexible inside. This property makes it ideal for use between materials that are constantly expanding and contracting, usually at different rates. A properly calked joint should last for many years.

Before calking, the surface should be cleaned, because the compound will not ad-

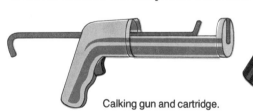

Calking gun and cartridge.

Scrape away old calking compound (left), and
then apply calking (right).

here properly where dirt or grease are present. Clean out loose dirt and debris with a wire brush. Scrape away old calking compound—it is a poor base for the new. If necessary, wash the area to be calked with a household detergent, but make sure that the surface is completely dry before applying the compound.

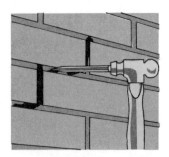

1. Chisel out loose mortar.

2. Wire-brush joint.

3. Trowel mortar into joint.

4. Form mortar.

When applying the compound, keep a smooth, even pressure on the gun's trigger. Run the gun along the joint in a single stroke without lifting to make a smooth, uniform bead. If you are doing the work in very cold weather, calking compound may become very stiff and difficult to handle. In this case, it is best to store the cartridge in a warm place for a few hours before using.

Calk around windows and doors and at all other places where different materials adjoin, such as where a plywood paneling abuts clapboard siding, or where shingles and brick are adjacent.

BRICK AND CONCRETE BLOCK

The most common problem in brick and concrete block walls is a defective mortar joint. The repair is simple. You can buy a prepared mortar mix at your hardware or building supply store. The tools required are a hammer (use either a ball peen or mash hammer—the claw hammer should be reserved for carpentry projects only), a cold chisel, a pointed trowel, and a wire brush. Chisel out loose or crumbling mortar, then clean the joint with the wire brush and wet it thoroughly. Mix the mortar, following the directions on the package. Force the mortar into the joint with the trowel, then form it with the point of the trowel to match the surrounding mortar joints. A

Making concave joint with a dowel.

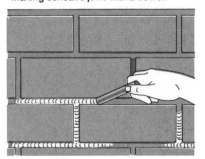

concave joint can be formed by using a dowel or a small piece of pipe to finish off the new mortar.

If a brick is loose or badly damaged, chisel out the mortar all around it, taking care not to damage the surrounding bricks. Take out the loose or damaged brick. Chisel away any remaining mortar in the opening and clean away dust and debris. Wet down the opening, then apply mortar to the sides and back. Dampen the replacement brick, coat it with mortar, and press it into place. Finish the mortar joint with a trowel.

If the mortar joints of an entire wall become porous, either because of age or because of poor original workmanship, the best solution is to apply a clear waterproofing compound (available at masonry and building supply stores) to each joint. This is a time-consuming task, but a necessary one. The alternative would be to completely remortar the wall.

On brick and other masonry walls, particularly new ones, a whitish powdery substance may develop. This is called efflorescence and is usually caused by the formation of salts in still-damp masonry. It can also be a sign of leakage. The deposit can be removed by scrubbing with a solution of one part muriatic acid to ten parts of water. Be very careful when working with this solution. Protect your skin and eyes with gloves and goggles. Work on small areas at a time, and flush frequently with clear water. Do not let the acid attack the mortar joints. If you accidentally get any of the acid on your skin, wash it off immediately.

In brick veneer walls, the brick is laid against a wood-sheathed wall behind it, attached by small metal clips. To allow proper drainage of this cavity, there are usually weep holes along the base of the wall to permit water to run off. Make sure that these holes are not blocked, either by dirt or fallen mortar, and clean them out occasionally with stiff wire or a masonry drill.

1. Remove damaged brick (above).

2. Apply mortar to cavity (above right).

3. Coat brick and place it into cavity (right).

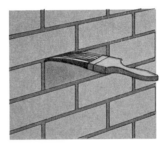

Apply waterproofing compound to each joint (left).

Brick veneer wall (below left).

Open weep holes (below).

CEMENT AND STUCCO WALLS

Stucco is a material made of cement, sand, and a small quantity of lime that is applied as a finish coating over concrete or

1. Clean away crumbling stucco.

2. Chisel stucco.

3. Undercut edges.

4. Trowel on new stucco.

First application below surface.

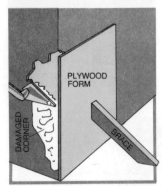

Outside corner repair, first stage.

Outside corner repair, second stage.

concrete block, or—less frequently—over wood or metal lathing. Cracks and gouges should be repaired quickly, to prevent their spreading due to the infiltration of water behind the coating.

First, wire-brush away the loose and crumbling material. If a larger area seems to be loose, use a cold chisel and hammer to clean off all the crumbling stucco. If in doubt, knock it out. Use the chisel to undercut around all the edges of the damaged area. Wet the area thoroughly, then apply a commercial mixture (available at your hardware store) to the area with a trowel, following the manufacturer's directions. Finish it, either rough or smooth, to match the surrounding stucco.

If the damaged area is quite deep—say 1½ inches or more—it is best to make the repair in two applications. Fill the hole with the compound to about ¼ inch from the surface. Allow the patch to dry for approximately 24 hours. Then finish it to the surface, as described above.

Outside corners are frequently damaged. The best way to get a good sharp corner repair is to do one side of the wall at a time. Prop a piece of plywood or lumber against the corner and pack in the stucco patch up to it. Allow it to dry, then move the form around to the other side of the wall and make the repair to the remaining damaged area. Make sure that the patches are allowed to dry thoroughly before removing the forms.

■Large damaged areas of stucco naturally require a bit more work. You may wish to leave such a repair to a professional, but it is still not beyond the reach of the do-it-yourselfer. You will probably have to take out all the damaged material down to the backing of lath or whatever. Wire-brush the area clean. Install new building paper against the backing, using rustproof nails. Nail a section of wire mesh against the backing. Three coats of stucco are best ap-

plied on such a repair. The first should be troweled over the mesh; scratch the surface with a scrap of the mesh to give "purchase" for the next coat. Allow it to dry thoroughly, at least 24 hours, and keep it damp during the drying period with an occasional spraying with a fine mist.

Apply the second coat to within ¼ inch of the surface, just as for a two-stage patch above. Allow it to harden for several days. Dampen the subsurface before applying the final coat. Trowel this to a smooth finish, flush with the surrounding stucco, and finish the surface to match. A whisk broom can be used to make a rough surface; a wooden trowel worked in a circular motion will give a smooth surface.

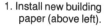

1. Install new building paper (above left).

2. Install wire mesh (above center).

3. Scratch surface of stucco patch (above right).

4. Spray during drying period (right).

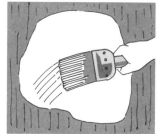

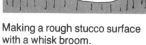

Making a rough stucco surface with a whisk broom.

Making a smooth stucco surface with a trowel.

SIDING

There is a wide variety of types, styles, and materials used as siding on frame houses. Generally, they can be broken down to shingle, clapboard, and panel types. Shingles may be of wood or asbestos cement. Clapboard, broadly speaking, may be wood, aluminum, hardboard, plastic, or steel. Paneling is most commonly plywood

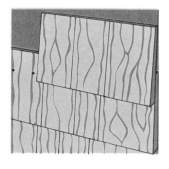 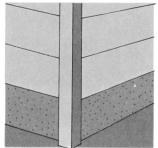 

Shingle, clapboard, panel siding (from left to right).

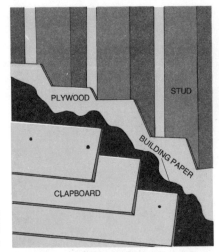

Shingle and clapboard installation.

Fill small cracks.

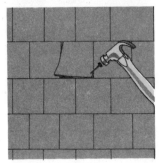

Secure loose board.

Drill pilot holes.

Countersink nails.

sheathing of boards, plywood, or composition material, with each course or row overlapping the one beneath it. Normally a paint job every couple of years is the only maintenance required. Faults may occasionally show up—cracks in boards or shingles, for example—or, where paint problems might exist (see CHAPTER 4), a board or shingle might become warped, blistered, or otherwise damaged.

Small cracks can be repaired by filling them with a lead-base putty. Work it into the crack with a putty knife. If a board or shingle has worked loose, secure it with galvanized or aluminum serrated nails driven along the edges. When you are repairing a material such as asbestos cement, which is very brittle, drill pilot holes for the nails before driving them. Nails can be countersunk and covered with putty. The putty is then painted over.

For wood siding split along the grain, pry up the loose portion of the board and apply a waterproof glue along the split. Press the split together and drive galvanized nails beneath the board to hold the edges together until the glue is dry. Then remove the nails and fill the holes with putty.

If a section of clapboard becomes damaged, you can replace it by first driving

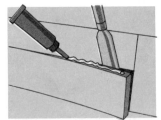

Glue split board.

Nail to hold together.

or hardboard, although plastic and some other materials are available. Patterns also vary greatly. But we can generalize with regard to repairs of damaged siding. No matter what the material, clapboard and shingle siding are applied over a tarpaper-covered

Chapter 3 • Exterior Walls

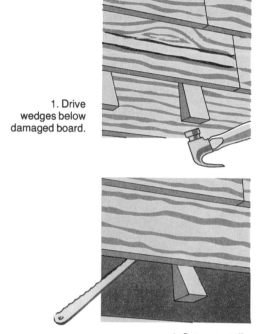

1. Drive wedges below damaged board.

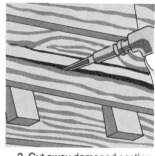

2. Cut away damaged section.

3. Put wedge under board above.

4. Cut away nails.

5. Tap new board in place.

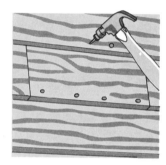

6. Nail new board in place.

wedges under the damaged section to separate it from the board below. Use a small handsaw, such as a back saw, to cut away the damaged portion. For added protection of the board below, wedge a flat piece of wood under the cut. When you have cut through the damaged board up to the board above it, move the wedges under the upper board. Then chisel away the damaged board. If the nail through the upper board passes through the damaged board, cut it away with a hacksaw blade, then remove the damaged section.

Use the damaged section of the clapboard as a pattern for cutting a replacement. Put the new board in place and tap with a hammer and a scrap of wood until it lines up with the boards on either side. Nail it approximately one inch from the bottom edge, then nail through the board above to secure the top of the replacement.

A warped shingle can sometimes simply be nailed back into place. Use serrated galvanized or aluminum nails, and use a nail set to avoid damaging the shingle while hammering. If a shingle is damaged or split and must be replaced, you must cut through the nail that holds it, which is concealed by the shingle that overlaps it above. You can do this by slipping a hacksaw blade under

To replace a damaged shingle, cut the nails first, then remove the shingle.

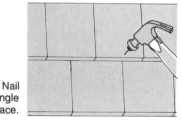

Nail replacement shingle in place.

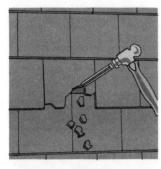

Break off damaged asbestos shingle.

Pull out exposed nails.

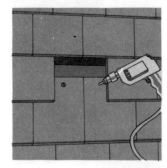

Drill nails through with electric drill.

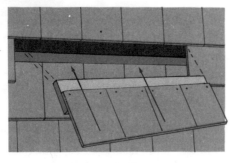

Replace shingle panel.

the shingle and cutting through the nail. Replacement shingles should be cut to fit tightly; this can be done with a utility knife. Nail through the shingle above and at the bottom of the replacement. The nails are countersunk and the holes filled with putty.

▲ Asbestos cement shingles that become cracked or otherwise damaged can be broken off piece by piece by striking them with a hammer and chisel. Just be careful not to damage the surrounding siding. Exposed nails can be pulled out with a pliers; nails of the shingle above are cut with a hacksaw. Another method is to drill them through from the outside. Slip the replacement shingle of the same size into position, and drill pilot holes for nails. Use a nail set to drive the nails home so that the hammer does not damage the asbestos shingle. Some asbestos shingles are attached to boards, usually about 4 feet in length. When one of these is damaged, it is generally best to replace the entire panel. This is done in a similar manner as replacing individual shingles.

When exterior paneling is used as siding, improper finishing may result in cracks or other paint problems. The latter are discussed in detail in the following chapter. Badly cracked paneling is best replaced. This can be quite a major undertaking, and one which you may prefer to leave to the professionals.

4

Proper Painting Practices

FOR SOME homeowners, painting the house's exterior is a perennial task and a year-round worry. It can be quite frustrating when you have spent large sums on the best paint money can buy and invested weeks of time in the painting process only to find a few months later that the paint is peeling, cracking, or, in general, not living up to expectations.

The source of the problem can usually be traced to faulty application and a lack of knowledge of the materials used. To save time and money, the homeowner may try to substitute one thick coat where two coats are recommended. Or, through inexperience, he or she may use the wrong primer (or no primer at all) and end up with unsatisfactory results. Mere cursory surface preparation before the paint is applied ususally makes itself apparent after a few weeks.

Even if the proper general procedures of house painting are observed throughout the project, faulty paint performance may still occur. The problems can arise from moisture resulting from poor rainwater drainage (see CHAPTER 2) or from overall climatic conditions. Paint will generally not last long in exceptionally humid areas. In arid regions, moisture is not usually a problem—but intense sunlight can be. In areas where there is little shade and the skies are clear most of the time, the continued exposure to the sun can result in a chemical breakdown of the paint and pigment fading.

The selection and application of exterior paint, therefore, should be based on the locale, as well as the paint's properties (ease of application, expected lifetime, color, etc.). Your paint distributor should have all the information you require along these lines.

In general, when choosing paint and primer, try to stick to the established name brands. Bargain paints may give poor results, and you must accept this risk when you use them. By investing in the better (albeit more expensive) tried-and-true brands, you are almost assured of uniformly high quality.

SURFACE PREPARATION

The condition of the surface to which exterior paint is applied is just as important as the quality of the paint. The surface should be clean, and defects that would adversely affect the paint should be repaired before painting is started. These defects include cracks in the surface, exposed nail heads, crumbled putty, rotted boards, pitted or corroded metal, mold, and mildew.

If peeling or flaking of the old finish has

Spot-paint surface
(above left).

Coat knots (above).

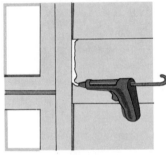

Calk gaps (left).

occurred, the paint should be removed and the cleaned area spot-painted. This includes building up the spot with primer and finish coats to the same level as the surrounding area. Knots should be coated with shellac or aluminum paint; decayed or split boards should be replaced (see CHAPTER 3); protruding nails should be countersunk and the holes filled with putty; as discussed in CHAPTER 3 gaps between ends of siding and corner boards or small cracks around window and door casings should be filled with calking compound.

To stop rot, liquid wood preservatives that can be applied by brushing, spraying, or dipping may be obtained at hardware and paint stores. The preservatives, which are sold under many brand names, contain either pentachlorophenol, copper naphthenate, or zinc naphthenate in a light volatile oil solvent. Pentachlorophenol solutions can be harmful to plants, so don't use them around shrubbery. The copper varieties may stain paint applied over them—a coat of sealer over these preservatives is advisable before painting. The more expensive zinc naphthenates are clear and can be applied under varnish for a natural wood finish.

Two coats of any of these preservatives are advisable, but one coat will give some protection. The second coat should be applied before the first is dry. One gallon usually covers up to 400 square feet of clean, dry, unpainted wood. All three preservatives are offensive to fungi that cause rot and unpalatable to boring insects such as ants, wood wasps, and powder post beetles. These insects should not be confused with termites, which require more positive control measures.

Preservatives should be used where wood touches the ground; in joints between wood and other building materials such as masonry, brick, concrete, or metal; in places where two pieces of wood fit tightly together; and in areas where moisture collects. Gloves should be worn when using the preservatives to avoid skin irritation.

Spray hard-to-reach spots.

Apply preservative to doorsill.

Apply preservative to garage door.

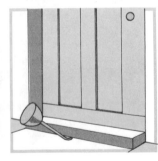

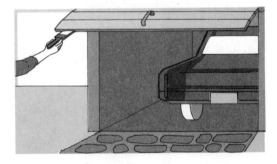

Places that are hard to reach are often the spots that need preservative most. To apply preservative to small, inaccessible joints such as in shutters or other outside blinds, use a fly sprayer, avoiding overdosage that might interfere with the movement of the slats. A bent-spout oil-can may also be used to apply preservative to the front edge and underside of a doorsill.

The bottom edge of a garage door is especially susceptible to rot and should be given a liberal coat of preservative, using a brush for an overhead door and an oilcan or absorbent pad for other types.

Badly mildewed surfaces should be washed prior to repainting with a solution of one pound of trisodium phosphate or sodium carbonate in one gallon of water. After thorough scrubbing, the areas should be rinsed with clean water and allowed to dry before painting. Commercial fungicides are available for controlling mildew on exterior painted surfaces.

PRIMERS

Primers for wood siding are of three general types: oil, fortified (made of oil and resin), and latex. The first two can be used if the house is to be painted with an oil-base paint. Only a latex primer may be used if the house is to have a latex-base top coat.

Oil primers contain oil to control wood penetration. The fortified primers are similar to oil primers, but because of the resins added to the vehicle they are faster drying and resist bleeding. The latex vehicle primers contain a little bit of oil to help develop sufficient adhesion, particularly over older surfaces.

CHOOSING PAINT

The old reliable type of paint to use is an oil base, since this type can usually cover an old finish in one coat, adheres well to most surfaces, and dries to a nice gloss. Oil-base paint will adhere only to a completely dry surface. Some oil-base paints contain mildew-resisting chemicals.

Latex paints are known by a variety of names but are always distinguished by the fact that they are water-thinned. These are very popular with the do-it-yourself public because of their quick drying, ease of clean-up, and relative lack of blistering and other problems caused by moisture. Another big plus for latex paint is that it can be applied on still-damp surfaces (after a rain or in the morning dew, for example), as compared with the waiting period required for an oil-base paint.

As a general guide, any wood siding can take an oil-base or a latex house paint. Vertical wood siding can use an oil-base, a latex, or a clear-finish paint. Wood shingles and shakes should be covered with latex and/or a clear finish. Use only latex on asbestos shingles. Downspouts can take either an oil-base or an alkyd enamel, which is a trim paint; the same is also true for metal gutters, metal windows, and doors. Use only an alkyd enamel on wood windows and doors, screens and storms, trim, cornice, and fascia. Aluminum siding and plastic siding take an oil-base house paint. The alkyd trim enamel is made from oil resins with a high proportion of fatty acids; this paint brushes on easily and retains its gloss very well. There are newer silicone alkyd trim enamels substantially more durable than the old type alkyd trim.

The clear finishes are sometimes preferred by those who want to retain the natural beauty of wood siding. No clear finish will be as durable as a pigment paint.

Stains can be used for wood shingles and rough siding and any outbuildings and fences that you plan to paint. Essentially these are heavily diluted linseed oil paints. If you are covering rough wood, stains are cheaper than paint and sometimes last twice as long.

Stir paint.

Add oil.

Pour paint back and forth.

Dip brush.

Tap brush.

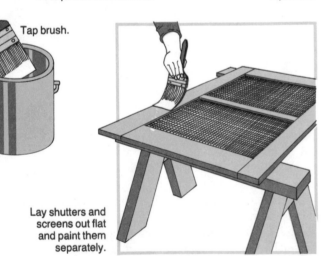

Lay shutters and screens out flat and paint them separately.

HOW TO PAINT

Once the preparation chores have been done and the proper primer has been applied according to the manufacturer's instructions, the house is ready for the top coat(s). Although paints are almost always mixed when you buy them, it is a good idea to stir them again before application. If the paint has settled (as is often the case with cans that have been around for a while), open the can and pour the surface oil into an empty, clean container. Stir up the pigment from the bottom of the original can until it is well dissolved, and then gradually pour back the oil while stirring. When all the oil has been returned to the original can, pour the paint back and forth from can to can until you are satisfied that the paint is thoroughly mixed.

When it is necessary to thin the paint, follow the manufacturer's label instructions to the letter. Paint can be ruined by the wrong oil or thinner. Add only a small amount of thinner at a time and continue stirring until it has been thoroughly absorbed into the paint.

Exterior painting should not be attempted when the temperature is below 50 degrees F. If you must paint in cool weather, be sure to stop at a time when the paint will have ample time to set before the temperature gets below 50 degrees. Don't paint in direct sunlight, as the paint will not dry properly and may develop hairline cracks.

Empty half the can into a clean receptacle. This will allow you to dip the brush without drowning it. The brush should be dipped in the paint only about 2 inches and then tapped against the side of the can to remove any excess. Do not pull the brush over the lip of the can, as this can damage the bristles of the brush.

Remove shutters, screens, and storm sash before painting; lay them out flat, and paint them separately.

Start at the highest point of the house and paint down to prevent drips and spatters from spoiling previously painted areas. If the gutters are to be the same color as the body of the house, paint them as you come to them. The trim areas (such as windows and doors) can be painted after the main body of the house unless they are to be painted the same color.

Paint large areas from side to side. It does not matter if you work from left to right or the reverse so long as you follow the sun around the house. Before you move or shorten your ladder, finish an entire area of 4 to 5 square feet.

Keep your trips up and down the ladder to a minimum by taking all the necessary equipment with you. You can use a hook to hold the paint can to a rung. If you're using a roller, special trays are available for this.

Ladders are vital painting tools. If they are not used properly they are also dangerous instruments. Check out the ladder safety principles discussed in CHAPTER 2. You should never attempt to paint higher than 4 feet above the top of the ladder, nor should you stretch out farther than you can reach with both feet firmly planted on the ladder. Also, never stand on the top rung of any ladder, including a stepladder.

Most painting is done in a horizontal direction, but shingles should follow the vertical grain. Professionals often do the high trim first to prevent the ladder from marring the body surface later on. On a very high place where one trip up the ladder is all you care to take, it is possible to do both the body and trim painting at one time if you are careful.

PAINTING MASONRY

Paints for masonry wall surfaces may be divided into four types: cement-water paint, resin-emulsion paint, oil paint, and paint containing rubber in the vehicle. These paints are suitable for use on such masonry surfaces as foundations, gate posts, and fence or enclosure walls, but they should not be used on floors that are subject to abrasion. Here, a very hard-drying paint with good water-resistance and gloss-retention is recommended.

Start at highest point.

Work from side to side.

Hook for paint can.

Don't overreach.

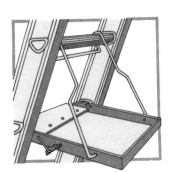
Roller tray.

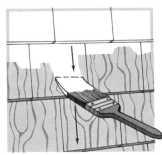
Paint shingles with grain.

Cement-water paints are water-dilutable paints in which portland cement is the binder. They are particularly suitable for application on damp, new, or open-textured masonry surfaces. These include walls that are damp at the time of painting, or that may become damp after painting as a result of structural defects; new structures (less than six months old) which normally contain water-soluble alkaline salts; and open-textured surfaces such as cinder, concrete, and lightweight aggregate block.

Close-textured surfaces that are relatively dry, such as cast concrete, asbestos-cement siding, and tile, may be painted with resin-emulsion paint or paints containing rubber in the vehicle. Walls that are dry at the time of painting, and are so constructed as to remain dry after painting, may be decorated with oil paints.

To clean a surface for the application of cement-water paint, thoroughly remove all dust, dirt, and efflorescence. Dust and dirt can be removed by brushing, followed by washing with clean water; efflorescence, old coatings of whitewash, and flaking or scaling cement-water paint are removed by brushing vigorously with a wire brush. (If efflorescence is stubborn, use methods detailed in CHAPTER 3.) Firmly adhering coatings of cement-water paint or cement-water paints that are "chalking" or "dusting" need not be removed, but should be brushed with a stiff-bristled brush to roughen the surface. If the old coating is organic paint, it must be completely removed. This can be done most effectively by sandblasting, normally a job for a professional.

Before applying the paint, whether initially or on a previously painted surface, masonry should be thoroughly wetted, preferably with a garden hose adjusted to produce a fine spray. A superficial dampen-

ing with a brush dipped in water is not adequate for exterior walls. Usually, wetting the walls not more than an hour before painting is sufficient. The water should be applied so that each part is sprayed three or four times for about 10 seconds, time being allowed between applications for the water to soak into the surface. If the surface dries rapidly, as it may in hot weather, it should be redampened slightly just before painting. The wall surface should be moist but not dripping wet when the paint is applied.

Cement-water paint powder should be mixed with water in accordance with the manufacturer's directions. Paints may be tinted by adding suitable amounts of coloring pigments, but, because of the difficulty of producing uniform colors by hand mixing, it is better to buy commercial brands of tinted paints that have been mill-ground in the factory.

Cement-water paint should be applied in two coats. Preferably not less than 24 hours' drying time should be allowed between coats. The first coat should be slightly moistened with water before applying the second.

Most portland cement paints cannot be satisfactorily applied with the ordinary hair-bristle paintbrush. Proper application requires a brush with relatively short, stiff fiber bristles such as fender brushes, ordinary scrub brushes, or roofers' brushes.

Although thick films are to be avoided, there is a tendency to use too much water in cement-water paint and to brush it out too

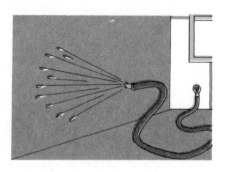

Wet masonry walls before painting.

Application of portland cement paint.

thin. Coatings applied in this manner may look well at first but generally lose their opacity and protective value much sooner than thicker films. The proper spreading rate is difficult to estimate for portland cement paint because of the differences in the textures of the masonry to be covered. On smooth masonry, one gallon of mixed paint should be sufficient to cover 100 square feet with two coats; for rough masonry, one gallon should be sufficient to apply two coats to 50 square feet of surface.

After painting, it is desirable to sprinkle the freshly painted surface two or three times a day with a fog spray, such as is used for dampening walls prior to painting; it is recommended that this be done between coats and for two days after the final coat, starting as soon as the paint has set, usually six to 12 hours after application.

METAL SURFACES

The chief reason for applying paint to exterior metalwork, particularly iron and steel, is to control and prevent corrosion. For best results, two coats of priming paint followed by two coats of top or finishing paint are recommended on new work. For repainting, a spot coat followed by a full priming coat, and then one or two finish coats, are recommended. The usual recommended spreading rate of each coat is about 600 square feet per gallon. The preparation of the surface, particularly steel, prior to painting is important. Unless the surface is properly cleaned so that the priming paint comes in direct contact with the metal, early failure of the paint film may occur.

All oil and grease should be removed first. The usual method is to wipe the surface with clean cloths and mineral spirits or carbon tetrachloride. The liquid as well as the cloths should be kept clean by frequent renewals to avoid leaving a thin, greasy film on the surface. When the oil and grease

Cleaning of metal surface with motor-driven rotary brush.

have been disposed of, rust, scale, and old paint may be cleaned from the surface with wire brushes, steel wool, or motor-driven rotary brushes.

The paint should be applied in bright, warm weather to metal surfaces that are clean and dry. Painting should not be done early in the morning when the surface to be painted is damp from dew. Ample time should be allowed for each coat of paint to dry before the next coat is applied.

Since the main function of a priming coat is to protect metal from corrosion, it should contain rust-inhibitive pigments. It can be applied by either brush or spray, but particular care should be taken to cover the surface completely with the proper thickness of paint. Two coats of primer are recommended for new work. The second coat may be tinted to a slightly different color to make sure of adequate surface coverage. Ample time should be allowed for drying before application of succeeding coats.

Two practical coatings for steel surfaces are red-lead and iron-oxide paints, red lead being used as a primer and iron oxide as a finishing material. Dull red and brown iron-oxide paints are economical for painting structural metal. They are durable and are frequently referred to as roof and barn paint.

As finish coats on iron or steel, black and dark-colored paints are more durable than light-tinted paints. Red-lead paint should not be used as a final coat, since it does not retain its color.

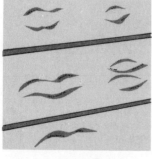
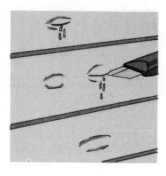

Blistering (above left).

Slit the bubbles with
a razor blade.

Scrape blistered area before
repainting (left).

BLISTERING

When the final coat has dried and the trim is completed, you will most likely find yourself with a satisfactory finish that will last for years with very little maintenance. Unfortunately, this is not always the case. Even with good paint and proper application, paint failures do occur, and moisture is often the culprit.

If you notice many bubbles, resembling blisters, on any outside painted surface of your house, chances are you have a blistering condition. One way to confirm this is to take a razor blade and slit a few of the bubbles. If blistered, the area beneath will feel wet, or water might actually seep out.

Blistering is caused by moisture accumulating behind the paint breaking its bond and shoving the film outward. If permitted to go too far, blistering could eventually break and lead to other more serious problems, such as peeling and cracking. To solve the problem, you must first determine where the excess moisture is coming from.

It can originate from outside or inside the house.

If blisters are localized around windows, dormers, or gutters and downspouts, then the condition is originating externally. Blisters around windows and dormers indicate that calking has probably cracked or failed, and water is penetrating beneath the paint.
● To correct this, do a thorough recalking job. Even when there is no sign of blistering, a home should be recalked before new paint is applied.

Blisters around gutters and downspouts generally indicate one of several problems: the gutters aren't pitched enough and water is overflowing during heavy rains; a gutter or downspout is damaged and leaking; or there's a damming condition (perhaps a downspout is clogged) that's causing water to back up and overflow. If you find this to be the case, repair the faulty downspout or gutter (see CHAPTER 2).

If the blistering is not localized but is found on large areas of the house, the moisture is probably coming from inside the house. The tremendous amount of moisture created in a modern home by clothes dryers, dishwashers, washing machines, sinks, showers, and cooking must get to the outside of the house one way or another. If a home isn't properly ventilated, this moisture goes through the walls but is stopped when it hits a nonporous oil-base paint film. The result is blistering.
▲ There are several ways to combat internal moisture so that it won't cause paint blistering. One is to apply latex paint to the house. This is a "breathing" paint that permits the moisture to escape through the paint film. However, before you apply latex paint to the house, all the old paint must be taken off. Ordinarily latex paint can be applied right over an oil-base paint, but the old paint will continue to block moisture from getting through.
▲ A better way to combat a buildup of in-

ternal moisture is to ventilate the home properly. Moisture-producing appliances such as clothes dryers should be vented to the outside. There should be adequate louvers in the attic; it is recommended that a home should have one square foot of louver for every 300 square feet of attic space.

After correcting the cause of the problem and before repainting, scrape and sand the blistered area smooth, then let it dry.

CHALKING

Under most conditions, chalking is normal and is the way in which paint ages. The paint film begins to disintegrate slowly and becomes powdery within a year or so after it has been applied. Chalking is usually desirable, since dirt and soot that settle on the house are washed off with the chalk when it rains, thus keeping the paint clean.

However, there may be abnormal or excessive chalking. This happens when paint begins to chalk too soon after it's ap-

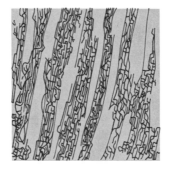
Checking.

Alligatoring.

plied or chalking proceeds at a very rapid rate, which means that the paint will have to be renewed more often than usual.

To avoid this problem, you should not try to make a can of paint go too far. Spread it on evenly and thick enough to cover the old surface. Also, if paint is applied in rain, fog, or mist, or if there is dew on the house, it could begin to chalk excessively. Another cause of abnormal chalking is applying only one coat of paint over a surface that is too porous.

Chalk-retardant paints are available and should be used where free chalking is not desirable. They last longer, but will not stay as clean. Chalk-retardant paint is particularly recommended for painting wood surfaces that are in contact with or above masonry. It prevents chalking runoff that will stain the masonry. This product is also recommended if a home is located in an area where heavy rains prevail.

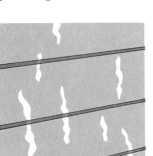
Chalking.

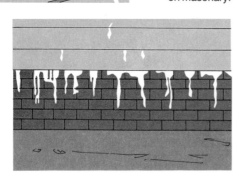
Chalking run-off on masonary.

CHECKING AND ALLIGATORING

If you find tiny, interlaced cracks appearing over the paint surface, it indicates a checking condition. Alligatoring is an advanced stage of checking in which the paint surface becomes interlaced with cracked lines over a large area and literally resembles an alligator's skin. If checking is noticed, it should be repaired before it reaches the alligatoring stage, which is followed by paint flaking off.

A major cause of checking is the application of a cheap paint that contains insufficient binder. Another cause is not allowing enough drying time between two coats of paint. If the first coat is not dry before the second coat goes on, it contracts and absorbs some of the binder of the second coat, causing checks to appear.

● If you encounter checking or alligatoring on any part of the house, scrape and sand the area smooth to eliminate the damaged paint before you repaint.

CRACKING

When this condition prevails, the paint cracks all the way down to bare wood, causing the paint film to curl up at the cracked edges.

Cracking can result from several causes. There may have been excessive moisture on the surface when the paint was applied, which led to blistering or peeling and finally to cracking. An inferior paint, lacking in elastic qualities, might have been used. The paint film must have sufficient elasticity to permit it to expand and contract along with the wood, or else cracking will occur.

Cracking can also result if paint isn't properly mixed before being applied or if it isn't brushed on evenly and smoothly. In these instances, oil and solid paint particles tend to clump together and can raise globules of paint in localized areas. Upon drying, the paint cracks and begins to curl.

Cracked paint should be removed down to bare wood before repainting. Never put new paint on top of it, because the top coat will only begin to crack again as the curled edges of the old paint push upward.

You should be aware of another type of cracking condition, particularly if you have an older home that has been repainted many times with oil-base paint. It's called cross-grain cracking—cracks appear across the grain of the wood. This indicates that too many thick layers of paint film have accumulated and they are too stiff to accommodate the normal shrinking and swelling of the wood underneath. Too much paint is often worse than too little paint. When this occurs, you have only one choice: remove all the old paint down to bare wood and start over again. No more paint than is necessary to restore the desired appearance should be used for repaint jobs. Paint that is in good condition, but dirty, should be washed occasionally rather than repainted.

CRAWLING

When you begin to paint and you notice that the paint is drawing itself up into drops or globules soon after it's applied, stop!

Cracking.

Cross-grain cracking.

Crawling.

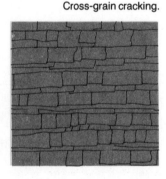
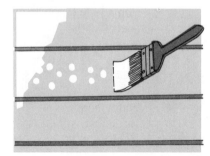

This condition is called crawling, and if you continue the globs will dry and then begin to crack.

Consider these questions, which will lead you to the cause of the crawling: Is the weather chilly or foggy? Are you using a rubber-base paint directly on top of an oil-base paint without a primer? Did you mix the paint thoroughly to distribute liquid and solid particles evenly. Did you use a paint remover on the surface before painting that left the surface greasy or waxy?

To prevent crawling, you should paint on a clear, dry day with the temperature no lower than 50 degrees. Mix the paint properly. If you must paint over a greasy or waxy surface, rub that surface with turpentine and steel wool, and then apply a bonding primer before putting on the finish coat. And don't mix paint with different kinds of bases.

FADING

All colored paint eventually fades. There are certain factors, however, that dictate whether some will experience this color failure faster than others. The paint on homes near bodies of salt water, for example, will fade much faster, because the salt air affects paints adversely.

If one side of your home is particularly subjected to heavy poundings of wind-driven rain and snow and then bright sunlight, it will fade faster than the other sides of the house. You don't have much control over salt or heavy weather conditions, but keep in mind that cheaper paints fade faster than more expensive types because they contain less or cheaper color pigments.

BLEEDING

This type of stain occurs most frequently on natural redwood or cedar siding and shingles. The soluble color or sap of the

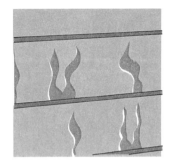
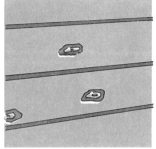

Bleeding (above).

Bleeding knots (above right).

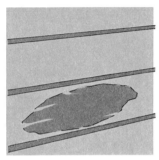

Creosote bleeding (right).

wood begins to run (or bleed), and the siding or shingles are stained. Usually the trouble arises from inadequate sealing of the wood due to thin paint films or irregular application. This allows moisture to penetrate the wood and extract the dye.

The way to stop this action is to apply a coat of shake-shingle paint to the surface to help prevent water penetration. If the siding or shingles have a natural finish, a coat of spar varnish will help. Sometimes excessive moisture originating from inside the house is the source of trouble, in which case corrective measures should be taken to reduce this moisture (see BLISTERING in this chapter).

If the bleeding is caused by knots in the wood, the stained areas should be sanded or scraped clean, than coated with a knot sealer and a top coat of paint to match the surrounding surface.

An altogether different type of bleeding action can result if the siding has originally been treated with creosote or with a paint containing creosote. You can detect it by noticing staining blotches, instead of runs, coming up through the paint. It means that the creosote has dissolved and is working its way to the surface.

To combat creosote bleeding, each blotched area should be scraped and sanded down to bare wood. The wood should be painted with a clear sealer or aluminum paint primer and then with two top coats. If the blotches are extensive, it might be necessary to do this to the entire house.

WRINKLING

When paint assumes a rough, wrinkled texture, the condition is known as wrinkling. The main cause is application of too thick a coat. Never try to make one coat of

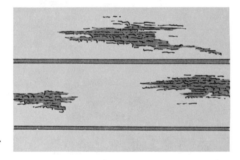

Wrinkling.

paint do the work of two, since the top surface will dry first and leave the bottom still soft. As the bottom surface attempts to dry, it can absorb the binder of the top paint and make that paint wrinkle. Wrinkling can also occur if paint is applied to a cold surface. In this case, only the top surface dries while the colder bottom surface remains soft.

MILDEW AND SULFIDE DISCOLORATION

These two conditions resemble each other. They take the form of rusty or sooty deposits on the paint surface.

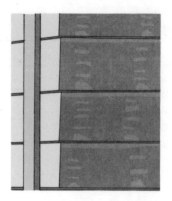

Mildew discoloration.

Mildew occurs primarily in damp climates, but it can form anywhere if a portion of the house doesn't receive sunlight. Suppose, for example, a corner is monopolized by shrubs that keep the siding in shade continuously. This spot is wide open to an attack by mildew-producing fungi.

Industrial chemicals carried in the air are the leading cause of sulfide discoloration, but this type of paint failure is not necessarily confined to those homes located in or near industrial sites. Sulfide discoloration can also occur in locations where there is rotting vegetable or animal matter, as near a stagnant beach area or swamp.

To treat the condition, you must first determine whether it is mildew, sulfide discoloration, or just plain dirt. Dirt can be washed off with a strong detergent—mildew and sulfide discoloration cannot.

To test for mildew, apply household bleach to a spot. If the area is mildewed, the bleach will lighten it. You can get rid of fungus by scrubbing the affected area with a solution of trisodium phosphate (available in paint stores) mixed in household ammonia and water, followed by a thorough rinsing with water. Then look over the area and determine if you can get some sunlight on it. Perhaps a rearrangement of one or two shrubs will suffice.

The test for sulfide discoloration is to wash the spot with hydrogen peroxide. If the stain lightens or bleaches, a sulfide condition exists. Hydrogen sulfide stains can be removed by a hydrogen peroxide solution, but the results are rarely worth the effort. The best solution is repainting.

When it's time to repaint and mildew or sulfide discoloration has been present, you should use a special fume- and mildew-resistant paint that will combat the condition. This type of paint contains no pigments that will discolor when exposed to hydrogen sulfide and also has a fungicide such as a phenyl mercuric compound added to it.

PEELING

Peeling can take place between the top coat of paint and the paint surface directly underneath it, or the entire paint film can peel away, exposing the bare wood. Peeling between coats is usually caused by the application of paint to a greasy or oily surface. It can also be caused by painting over an area that is too smooth or glossy, as is frequently the case under eaves where the old coat of paint was protected from normal weathering.

●Before repainting, always roughen hard glossy surfaces with sandpaper and remove loose flakes of old paint where peeling has occurred. Greasy or oily material should be removed by washing with a detergent, wiping with solvent, or sanding.

If peeling occurs between the paint film and the wood surface, it is usually the result of a moisture problem. Often, paint blisters caused by moisture break open, and the paint film flakes off. The moisture problem should be cured before painting (see BLISTERING in this chapter).

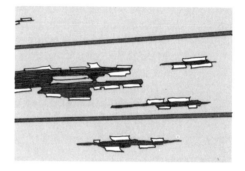

Peeling.

5

Doors and Windows

EXTERIOR DOORS take a lot more of a beating than do those inside the house. They are exposed to the elements, and they are operated—opened and closed—more frequently than most doors inside the house, with the possible exception of bathroom doors. They are more likely to be slammed shut by youngsters (and adults) in a hurry than are other doors. Windows, too, are subject to a lot of abuse, from the elements, and from frequency of raising and lowering or otherwise opening and closing.

Doors and windows can be the weak spots on the outside of your home. Obviously a broken window will not do its job of keeping out the elements, although its other function of letting in light will still be performed—except that you will probably have more light than you care for in such a situation. A door that does not close properly or fits poorly will also not perform as it should and will admit unwanted drafts and insects. It's just common sense to keep doors and windows in good shape.

PREVENTIVE MAINTENANCE

The old aphorism about "a stitch in time" definitely applies here. One "stitch" is to make sure that all exterior doors are hung on three hinges. Interior doors are normally hung on only two hinges, which are enough to support this weight. But exterior doors are of heavier construction, and the third hinge located midway between top and bottom hinges is necessary to support this additional weight; without a third hinge, the door is likely to bind and scrape.

It's also important to keep those hinges swinging freely by lubricating them periodically. You can use household liquid or stick lubricant or machine oil, and while you're at it, give a shot to the door-latching mechanism as well, working the doorknob back and forth as you do. For lock mechanisms, an occasional treatment with graphite should keep them working smoothly.

Windows, too, should be routinely maintained. Sash pulleys and channels should be lubricated. Hinges on casement windows

Exterior doors should be hung on three hinges.

Lubricate hinges and latches periodically.

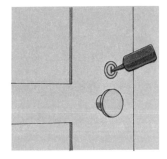

Lubricate locks with graphite.

Lubricate hinges on casement windows (below). Lubricate sash pulleys (right).

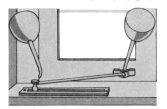

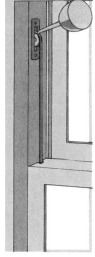

pearance of new aluminum. After cleaning the surface thoroughly with a good-quality scratchless cleanser to remove every last trace of dirt, oil, or grease, coat the surface with a rustproof finish.

STICKING DOORS

Dampness causes wood doors to swell and stick. As the air dries out, the wood shrinks and the door will once again operate freely. Therefore, planing a sticking door should be a last resort.

Check the condition of the hinges. Position yourself on the inside of the door (so that it closes away from you). With the door closed, examine the spaces between the door and frame. You can run a sheet of paper around the edges to observe the hang of the door; where it binds, the door is too tight. If there is a space at the top, latch side of the rail and a corresponding space at the bottom, hinge side, it means that the upper hinge is probably loose and perhaps the middle and lower ones as well.

Open the door to expose the hinges. Relieve pressure on the top hinge by having someone lightly support the door by its handle, or by slipping a wedge of some sort under the bottom rail. Use a screwdriver to

should be lubricated, as well as the winding mechanisms. Locks should be kept clean and lubricated so that they operate easily.

Paint on both windows and doors should be kept up, and renewed every two to three years at least on the outside. When painting windows, make sure that you don't "paint them shut." Free them as soon as the paint has dried (see page 54).

Steel window casements present other maintenance problems. Many basement windows and other window sashes are of steel. Rain, snow, sun, and constant change in temperature make them prime targets for the invasion of rust. You should keep the outside surfaces of steel windows in good shape by coating them with a rust protector. If they are already rusty, remove scale and loose rust by scraping and wire-brushing. Then apply a special primer over the cleaned surface. Follow this with a coat of rust-proofing finish.

Aluminum doesn't rust, because rust is the oxide of iron. But aluminum does oxidize, into a whitish film that dulls its surface and certainly detracts from the appearance of your home if you have aluminum windows. You can preserve the silvery ap-

Check hang of door with a sheet of paper.

Slip wedge under door while tightening hinge screws.

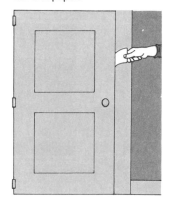

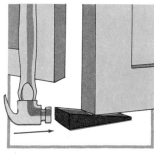

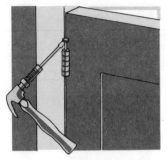

Knock out hinge pins (middle pin first, top pin last).

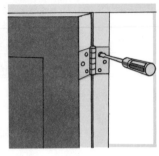

Remove hinges if pins are "frozen."

Hammer in wooden plugs.

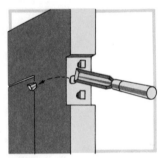

Trim plugs.

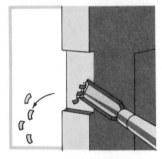

Chisel mortise deeper.

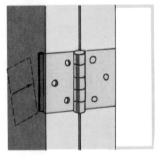

Build up hinge with a shim.

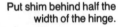

Put shim behind half the width of the hinge.

Reposition hinge leaf in its mortise.

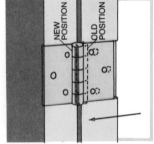

tighten all the screws. If a screw does not appear to have any purchase, the wood around the screw has deteriorated. This can be corrected.

Remove the door by knocking out first the middle then the lower and upper hinge pins. Use a screwdriver angled so that the head of the pin is driven up and out. Should the pin be "frozen," remove the hinge at the jamb. Inspect the mortise and the condition of the wood. If the holes look pulpy or rotted, hammer in a small wooden plug coated with glue or stuff the spaces with toothpicks or wooden matches dipped in glue. Trim, then replace the hinge, using longer screws if possible.

▲Sometimes the hinge plate is not recessed deeply enough in the mortise, in which case you will have to chisel the mortise deeper. Or it may be possible, if spacing at the latch stile permits, to build up the lower and middle hinges and thus shift the door to the vertical. The shim can be any piece of cardboard of the correct thickness (a matchbook cover serves well) and it should fill the mortise completely.

▲When the door binds along the entire length of the latch stile, you will have to cut the mortises deeper, as required. If necessary, you can deepen the mortises on both the jamb and the door.

●Shimming helps if the door tends to spring open when you try to close it. In this case, place a strip of cardboard behind only half the width of the hinge leaf. You need not remove the hinge for this operation. Loosen the screws so that when the door is partly closed, the hinge leaf comes away from the mortise. Slip the shim into this space and tighten the screws. Shimming at this point serves to change the angle of the door so that it leans toward the stop.

▲If the hinge stile is catching or binding along the stop, you can reposition the hinge in its mortise to pull the door away a bit.

Often a door binds at several points at once because it or the frame has been warped out of shape. (Cracks or stress marks on the interior wall around the frame are signs that the frame is at fault). In this case, adjusting the hinges will not do the job completely. You will have to plane or sand the door as well.

Careful inspection will show where excess material has to be removed. Usually only a portion of an edge has to be corrected, rather than the entire length of a stile or rail. If such is the case at the outside stile, you can probably get away without having to remove the door.

Mark off the sticking areas while the door is closed so that you know how much has to be cut. Remove the door if necessary and prop it on its edge against some solid support. Work the plane in smooth strokes and do not bite too deeply at any one time. If the binding exists at the latch area of the door it may prove simpler to plane the hinge side instead. Hinge leaves are easier to remove than the lock assembly.

▲ When the door rubs at the top or bottom, you must plane one or both rails, either partially or fully. Here you are cutting across the grain, and if you work too roughly or use a dull tool it is easy to splinter the wood. If the amount to be removed is minimal, use a sanding block instead, but take care not to bevel the door edges.

▲ A door sometimes becomes too narrow because of shrinkage, with the result that the latch is not able to reach the striker plate to engage it. In this case, build up the width of the door by gluing and nailing a

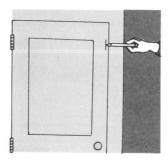
Close door, mark sticking areas.

Remove door and plane.

Plane rail.

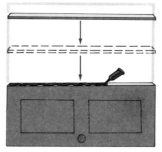
Glue wood strip to stile.

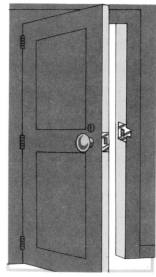
Mark striker plate, close door.

Plane stile without removing door.

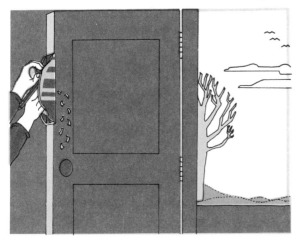

strip of wood along the hinge stile. Measure to determine where the hinge leaves should be set, and chisel new mortises to receive them. Finish the strip to match the door.

▲ These adjustments may create a problem. The door now swings freely but the latch is unable to engage the striker plate in the frame, with the result that the plate must be repositioned. To tell how much and in what direction, rub some crayon over the face of the striker plate and close the door. The resultant mark on the plate will indicate what has to be done.

If the latch is centered but falls short of

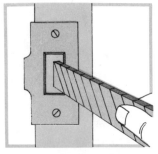

File striker plate.

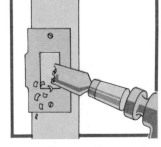

Trim wood from mortise.

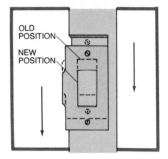

Move striker plate.

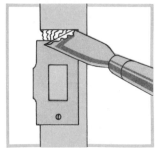

Fill depth with wood putty.

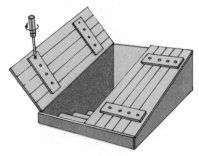

Temporary repair of basement entry door.

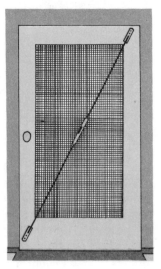

Correct sagging screen door.

the receptacle in the plate, try filing the metal to align the hole. Also trim wood from the mortise, if required. If the entire plate has to be moved, fill the original screw holes with plugs before attempting to screw the plate in a new position. Gaps between the plate and the mortise can be filled with wood putty and touched up with paint. These same instructions apply when the plate must be moved up or down to meet the latch.

● Because they are of lighter construction than standard doors, screen and combination screen-and-storm doors sometimes sag or bend out of shape, making them difficult to close. This can be corrected by the use of a turnbuckle and cable placed on either the inside or outside of the door.

The cable should be long enough to fit from one corner of the door to the corner diagonally opposite, plus enough extra for connections (either by twisting or by the use of cable clamps). Cut the cable in half. Fasten one piece of the cable to a screw eye on the top side rail over the hinges; fasten the other to the bottom of the opposite side rail. Fasten the turnbuckle between the two cables. Tighten the turnbuckle until the door is squared up and closes properly.

▲ Outside basement doors or hatchways present some special problems because they are completely exposed to the weather and serve the function of a roof as well as a door. The old wooden types should be painted every year. As they deteriorate, you can make temporary repairs by screwing 1 x 3 or 1 x 4 cleats across the boards, preferably on the inside if this is possible. Eventually, though, the entire door will have to be replaced. The best choice here is a weather-tight steel door.

STICKING WINDOWS

When a wood window sash sticks or binds, it is often because of carelessly applied paint that has worked into the sash

Tap sash with a hammer and a block to free window.

If the tapping does not help, free window with chisel.

If this still does not work, pry window up from bottom.

Sand molding and track after window is free.

molding. Paint-stuck windows can often be freed by tapping along both sides of the sash with a hammer and a block of wood. If this doesn't work, insert the blade of a paint scraper or a broad, thin chisel (never a screwdriver, which would gouge the wood) between the sash and the stop molding inside the house. Rock the tool back and forth gently to force the sash back from the molding. Repeat this at several points at each side of the sash until it moves freely.

If the window still can't be raised, or if a seal forms at the bottom edge of the sash after painting, the window can be pried loose from the outside without damage to the finish. A hatchet is a good tool for this, or any broad, hard metal wedge. Hammer the tool along the bottom of the sash and pry as you go along.

Once the window is free, scrape off any crusts of paint at the back face of the stop molding. Sand the molding lightly, touching up the window track as well.

A window may also become permanently swollen out of shape. Try this repair first: Cut a block of wood that will fit snugly into the channel between the inner and outer window stops. Give the block several smart raps with a hammer at both sides of the window. This should free the sash so that it can be raised at least partially. Repeat the procedure at the exposed channels at the bottom. Then apply lubricant such as paraffin or candle wax to the channels.

If this method fails, the sash will have to be removed from the frame to make the necessary adjustments. The lower sash must be removed before the upper. Most newer windows are equipped with metal tension strips fastened to the channels. With some of this type, it is possible to remove the sash simply by pressing it sideways into a channel and lifting it free.

On windows with sash cords, the stop molding will have to be removed first. Insert a thin, broad chisel behind one end of the molding and twist so that the strip comes away partially at that point. Work

Hammer tapping block above window channel.

After window is raised, repeat procedure at the bottom.

Release sash from tension strips fastened to the channels.

Insert chisel behind one end of the molding.

Secure sash cord.

Disengage sash cord.

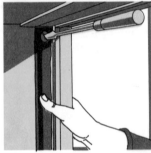

Adjust tension strips.

Plane sash.

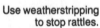

Use weatherstripping
to stop rattles.

Remove molding and nail it
back closer to the sash.

of oil to the pulley shaft (as you should be doing regularly anyway).

If the window has tension strips, try adjusting these first by turning the mounting screws. If this does not work, or if no mechanical adjustment is possible, wood can be sanded or planed from the sides of the sash to make it fit. Do not remove too much material at any one time. It is a good idea first to clean up and lubricate the channels, then check the fit of the window as you plane or sand. It should fit snugly without binding.

When a wood window rattles, there is too much space between the sash and its stop molding. An easy way to alleviate this problem is to run a strip of metal or felt weatherstripping into the space. To make a permanent repair, remove the molding and nail it back closer to the sash.

Metal sliding windows (such as aluminum storm windows) may bind when dirt collects in the tracks. Sometimes the metal becomes pitted, impeding the window's

Clean metal tracks
with steel wool.

Tighten loose
screws on hinges
of casement
windows.

carefully to avoid damaging or breaking the molding. With the strip removed, disengage the sash cord at each side. Fasten a nail or strip of wood to the ends of the cords so that they will not slip past the pulley. Lower the weight gently and observe the action of the pulley. If it is stiff, apply a few drops smooth operation. Usually this can be corrected with a cleanup and rubbing with fine steel wool. The tracks should then be lubricated periodically with paraffin or wax. Never try to pry the window with a sharp tool—this will distort the tracks.

When steel casement windows stick or bind, check to see that hinges are free of rust or accumulated paint. Look for loose hinge screws or for binding in the crank mechanism. Tighten hinges and clean with steel wool, then apply machine oil. It may be necessary to open the handle assembly for cleaning and oiling.

REPLACING BROKEN GLASS

The replacement of broken windows is the subject of frequent amusement in the funny papers, wherein the juvenile protagonist puts a baseball or football through the picture window of the neighborhood crabby old man. The humor is undeniable, but the reality isn't all that much fun.

Replacing cracked or broken window glass is not difficult, but it does require some care. You need a sharp glass cutter (if you cut the glass yourself), prepared putty or glazing compound (more flexible than putty), glazier's points, pliers, and a putty knife.

Installation of the glass is normally done from the outside, so if you are repairing a second-floor window it may be wise to remove the sash, if that is possible. Wear heavy work gloves when removing broken pieces of glass from the frame. Heat from a soldering gun will help soften the old putty, or a small wood chisel can be used to clean it out, but take care not to damage the frame. Extract the metal glazier's points with pliers.

The replacement glass should be cut $1/16$ inch smaller all around than the frame opening, to allow for any irregularities that may exist in the frame. Most hardware stores will cut glass to specified size, or you can do it yourself as follows.

Mark the glass with a sharpened crayon, then turn it over and lay it on a flat surface covered with newspaper or an old blanket. Use a steel straightedge to guide the cut. Any doubts about the condition of the glass cutter can be satisfied by first scoring a piece of the old glass: if the score mark shows signs of skipping, the cutting wheel is dull or chipped. You might as well scrap it and buy a new one—it's a lot cheaper than ruining a piece of glass.

Make sure the glass is free of dust or grit before attempting the cut. The score mark should be begun at the edge of the glass farthest from you, then followed through in a single motion with smooth, even pressure on the cutter. When the glass is scored, lay it over the straightedge or the edge of a table and apply pressure on both sides of the score to break it cleanly. If the piece to be

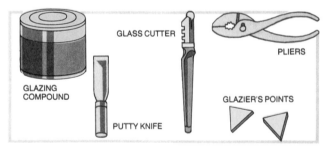

Tools to replace broken glass.

1. Score glass.

2. Break glass along score mark.

3. If the strip is narrow, break it off with glass cutter.

4. Apply bed of glazing compound before installing the glass.

5. Press glass into frame.

6. Install glazier's points.

7. Press in glazing compound.

8. Smooth with putty knife.

removed is very narrow, snap it off with the slotted head of the cutting tool.

Before installing the glass, apply a ⅛-inch bed of glazing compound around the rabbeted groove of the frame. Press the glass into place, making sure it lies flat against the shoulders of the frame. Secure it with the glazier's points, pressing them into the frame 4 to 6 inches apart on all sides.

Make a "rope" of glazing compound about ½ inch thick. Use your fingers to press it against the wood and glass around the frame. Smooth and bevel the compound with the blade of the putty knife, making sure you leave no breaks or separations in the seal. A coat of paint finishes the job.

For metal windows the procedure varies slightly. On these the glass panes are secured to the frames with small metal clips buried in the compound. These will have to be removed and set aside. Lay a bed of glazing compound into the frame and set the replacement glass firmly into this bed. Install the clips, then apply the final bed of glazing compound.

Metal storm windows normally have frames that are grooved to hold a gasket that secures the glass in place. This is removed when glass must be replaced. The new glass is inserted into the channels of the frame. The gasket is then pressed back into place.

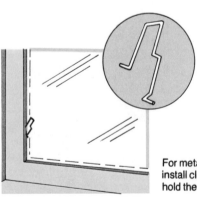

For metal frames, install clips to hold the glass.

Insert new glass into storm window frame (left) and press gasket into place.

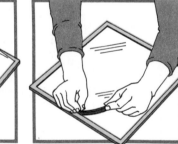

There have been numerous instances of people seriously injuring themselves by walking through or putting their hands through large windows or doors. Safety and consumer agencies have been urging legislation requiring the use of less hazardous materials in such vulnerable places as sliding glass patio doors, storm doors, and other areas where glass might be a hazard.

Laws incorporating these recommendations have already been passed by several states, requiring that "safety glazing material" be used in potentially dangerous areas. Some of the safety materials are tempered glass, laminated glass, wire glass, and acrylic plastic.

These materials may be slightly more difficult to install than regular glass, and their cost is generally higher. By installing these materials in place of standard glass panes, however, the extra cost will be offset by the sense of security in knowing one's house is safe. One thing to watch out for with the rigid plastic materials such as acrylics is surface mars. While their lesser hardness makes them less susceptible to breakage than glass, it also increases their chances of getting nicked or scratched.

SCREEN REPAIR

Keep wood window and door screens in good condition by stacking them flat in a dry, well-ventilated area until ready for use. Frames should be tightened when necessary and given a fresh coat of paint from time to time to help preserve them.

A damaged wood screen frame can be repaired easily enough. Trouble usually occurs at the frame joints. The joint itself may be loose or the wood broken or rotted. A joint can be tightened by bracing the frame pieces with ⅜ inch dowel. Drill a hole though the side member into the top or bottom piece, or, if the corners are mitered, at an angle through both pieces. Coat the

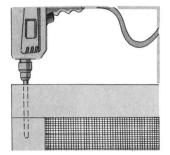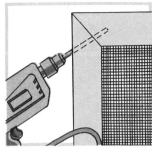

1. Drill a hole into the frame joint of the screen.

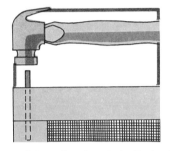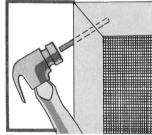

2. Drive a dowel, coated with glue, into the hole.

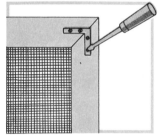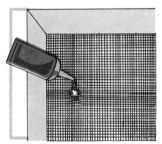

Repair of the frame joint with a flat metal angle.

A drop or two of waterproof cement will cover a small hole.

dowel with glue and hammer it into the hole, trimming or driving it flush, as the case may be. Another method is to fasten a flat metal angle over the corner joint. This type of repair is more noticeable, however.

A small hole in screening should be patched as soon as it is discovered. Otherwise, it is an invitation to tiny bugs, and it will almost surely grow rapidly in size. If the hole is small enough, a drop or two of waterproof cement will do the job. The cement hardens and covers the hole.

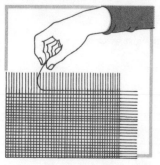

1. Unravel wires on patch.

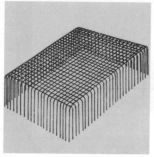

2. Bend wires.

3. Insert over damaged area.

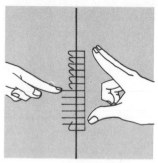

4. Bend back wires.

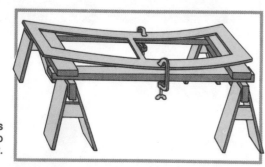

Clamp frame across sawhorses to assure tight fit.

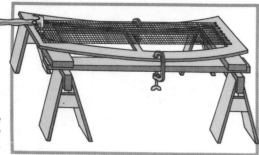

Tack new screening tautly at each end.

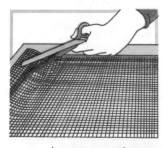

Lay new screening over metal frame.

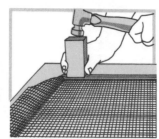

Tap spline back into its groove.

For larger holes and tears, use a snips or heavy-duty scissors to cut a patch of wire screen material ½ inch larger than the hole. If you do not have extra screen, patches in various sizes are available at any hardware store.

Unravel two wires at each side of the patch, then bend the end wires at a right angle on all four sides. Place the patch over the hole and push the bent wires through to the other side of the screen. Then bend them back to secure the patch firmly.

When screening is badly damaged or deteriorating, replacement is necessary. To replace wire screen in a wood frame, first remove the molding. Use a paint scraper or putty knife for this job, prying gently along the length of the molding until it comes free. Remove all staples or tacks from the frame and take out the old screening. Cut the new screen 1 inch wider at all sides with scissors or snips.

To assure a tight fit, apply tension to the screen while it is being tacked to the frame. The best way to do this is to lay the frame across a pair of sawhorses or a work surface as wide as the frame. Place a cross board under each end of the frame, then C-clamp the sides of the frame to the work surface so that there is a slight bow formed in the middle.

Tack the new screening tautly at each end, doubling the material where you tack. Now release the C-clamps and tack the screen along the sides of the frame. Replace the molding and trim any wire that protrudes from under it.

In metal frames, a spline holds the screening in place. This must be pried out to remove torn screening. New screening is then laid over the framing and trimmed to size, with the corners cut at 45-degree angles. The spline is then tapped back into its groove in the frame to secure the screening.

6

Porches

Porches are things of the past. Once people began jetting around in auto-mobiles and watching television, there was little need to pass the time waving to neighbors while rocking on the front porch. Plenty of older homes still have them, however, and their owners cherish them on balmy summer evenings when the mock-orange is in fragrant bloom.

Practically speaking, however, a porch can often be a liability rather than an asset. Most porches around today have long been exposed to the elements and often show signs of decay. Many homeowners resolve this problem by either removing or closing in their porches. To nostalgia buffs, this is heresy, but we can sympathize.

SAGGING PORCH

If a porch has a major problem, it is usually manifested by sagging. This means that one or more of the structural members has deteriorated, usually because of excess moisture. The underside of a porch is much like the crawl space of a home, except that it is not as completely enclosed and the usual moisture-preventive steps have not been taken. Use the same preventive methods on porch crawl spaces as for those under the house itself.

Staple a vapor barrier to the underside of the porch floor joists, after first making any necessary repairs to structural members (see below). Cover the ground beneath the porch with polyethylene sheeting or heavy felt paper, overlapping the seams and the house wall 3 or 4 inches and sealing all seams and the wall joint with asphalt cement. Then spread a 2-inch-thick layer of sand over the area.

You'll have to get in under the porch to take these measures, of course, which may mean removing latticework, or perhaps some of the masonry that forms the foundation of many porches. If you're lucky, it will be only latticework, because you may cause more problems than you solve by blasting through masonry.

Once inside, you may find some company. Rats, mice, cats, and other animals love

Staple vapor barrier beneath joists.

Cover ground beneath porch with sheeting.

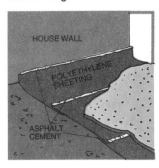

Raise the porch flooring
with a brace.

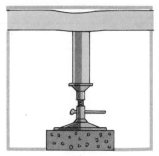

Raise the porch flooring
with a jack.

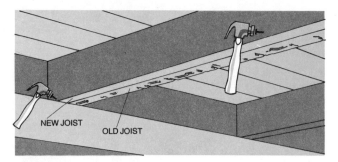

NEW JOIST   OLD JOIST

Nail new joists next
to the old ones.

Nail floor boards to joists
from above.

the cozy space under a porch. So take a flashlight—and maybe a baseball bat. Check all the wood beams and joists. Some may be obviously decayed, others less obviously so. Dig a penknife into all of the structural members to see if they are in good shape or not.

Most sag problems can be cured by running new joists next to the old ones, but first you have to get the porch up to the right level. Unlike the structural members of the main part of the house, there isn't usually much weight bearing on the joists,

so try to raise the flooring with a piece of 4 x 4 or 2 x 4, braced against a solid surface below. If that doesn't work, rented adjustable jacks should do the job.

Once the floor is level again, nail new joists next to the old, driving nails into both the old joists and the beams on each end. Afterwards, nail the floorboards down into the new joists from above.

If the main beams or supports of the porch are also in poor condition, you can try buttressing them as with the joists. This may not be possible, in which case you don't have much choice except to remove the porch entirely. You can build a new one if you're "into" porches, but economically it's not too wise.

REPLACING DAMAGED FLOORBOARDS

There is no reason why porch flooring shouldn't last as long as the other wood in a home. If kept painted with a good porch-and-deck paint, and if moisture doesn't collect underneath, the boards should endure. But if this painting is neglected, and moisture problems in the crawl space are also ignored, rotted floorboards are likely.

Most porch flooring is of the tongue-and-groove variety. When replacing damaged sections, it is important not to mar the surrounding boards. The section must be cut away over the nearest joists. To replace just a board or two, mark off the section of board to be removed at an exact right angle to the boards. A framing square will help here. With an electric drill or brace and bit, make large, interconnected holes inside the lines on both ends of the damaged section. With a large wood chisel, break out the damaged portion by striking along the grain.

Remove the pieces, being particularly careful not to damage the tongue or groove

1. Mark board over joists.

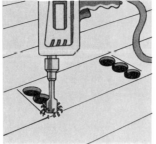

2. Drill holes.

3. Chisel along grain.

of the boards on either side. Chisel out the remainder of the board on the outside of the drilled holes, making sure that you cut exactly on the line. Pull out any remaining nails and clean out all debris.

Now put a new board along the removed section, and mark carefully where the damaged section was, again at an exact right angle using the framing square. Saw along the lines and chisel off the *bottom* of the grooved edge so that the board will slip into the open space. (Leave the top portion of the grooved edge.) Slip the board into place and nail through the top with aluminum or galvanized flooring or finishing nails. Use two nails on each end, set them, and cover with wood filler.

RAILING REPAIRS

Porch railings also suffer from the elements and neglect. Replacement is routine, by removing the rotted rail or baluster and replacing with a new one—if you can find a matching piece. It may be impossible to find a matching baluster for many old-fashioned railings, and a new one may have to be fabricated. You can do this yourself if you have a lathe. Otherwise, take the old one to a millworking shop and have a new one turned. The joints on exterior work are usually simple, and you should be able to knock out the deteriorated pieces with a

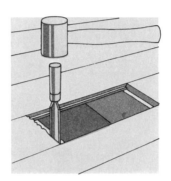

4. Chisel at ends.

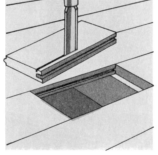

5. Mark new board.

6. Remove bottom of grooved edge.

7. Fit new board into place.

8. Nail securely.

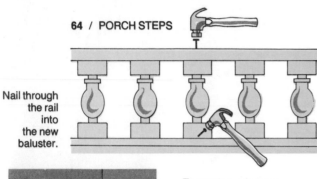

Nail through the rail into the new baluster.

hammer and replace them without complicated joinery by nailing through the rail into the baluster, or toenailing the baluster to the rail.

PORCH STEPS

If porch treads are simply worn down, the easiest way to repair them is to pry them up with a wrecking bar, turn them over, and nail them in place bottomside up. Outside steps are not ordinarily rabbeted or dadoed. Use aluminum or galvanized finishing nails, set the nails, and fill the holes with wood putty.

When new treads or risers are needed, take an old one to the lumberyard and try to find a match. If you can't match exactly, buy lumber of a greater width and rip to fit. (Today's dimensional lumber is slightly thinner than that of times past, but this need be of no concern, as the structural strength is essentially the same, or greater.) Rounded edges can be duplicated with a rasp and sandpaper. Apply wood preservative to new wood before nailing in place.

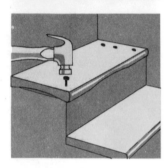

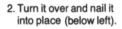
To repair porch steps:
1. Pry up worn tread (left).

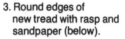
2. Turn it over and nail it into place (below left).

3. Round edges of new tread with rasp and sandpaper (below).

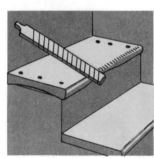

Chapter 6 • Porches

7

Driveways and Sidewalks

ALTHOUGH DRIVEWAYS and sidewalks can be made of a variety of materials such as brick, stone, or gravel, most are composed of concrete or blacktop (asphalt). There is no such thing as a "cement" driveway. Cement is merely a small (though very important) ingredient in a concrete mix.

Concrete is made up mostly of "aggregate" (crushed stone or other inorganic matter) and sand, mixed with cement and water. In a very real sense, cement is the "glue" that holds the mixture together. When mixed with water, it is called by the accurate and descriptive phrase "cement paste."

The cement used in concrete is portland cement, a soft, fine, grayish-green powder made from pulverized limestone and other ingredients. The term portland was applied because the concrete made from it resembled Portland stone, a widely used building material of the 19th century.

The usual concrete mix for driveways and sidewalks is roughly 10 percent portland cement, 17½ percent water, and 72½ percent sand and medium-size aggregate. Concrete mixes can vary from a lean, stiff mix of 15 percent water, 7 percent portland cement, and 78 percent sand and large, coarse aggregate to a rich, wet mix of 20 percent water, 14 percent portland cement, and 66 percent sand and small, fine aggregate. The aggregates are broken down into fine, medium, and coarse. Sand is actually a very fine aggregate, as is crushed gravel. Coarse aggregate is usually crushed stone, but it can also be gravel or blast-furnace slag.

There are quite a few important steps involved in laying long-lasting concrete, and if any of them are omitted or skimped on, the result can be flaking, scaling, or some other form of deterioration. Concrete that has been carefully mixed, placed, and cured should last several lifetimes. But even when it is perfectly constructed, a sidewalk or driveway has several natural enemies—trees, children with hammers, and frosts, to name just a few.

MINOR CONCRETE REPAIRS

The art of concrete repair has advanced greatly in the past decade or so. New repair mixes containing a vinyl or epoxy ingredient have made minor repairs quick and easy. Except for large cracks, special patching mixes are recommended rather than the standard concrete formula. Standard concrete does not adhere well to old concrete.

Patching compounds can be "feathered" to smooth edges, which makes them ideal

Feather edge of patch.

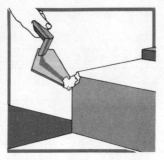

Repair step corner.

same when he puts a filling in a tooth.) This provides "tooth" for the concrete patch. A standard concrete mix is then pressed into the crack with a trowe or similar instrument. Most building supply houses sell small bags or pails of premixed concrete for this purpose. Or you can mix your own, as described later for major repair work.

for repairs that need a fine edge. They can also be applied on top of old concrete without elaborate preparation. Vinyl or epoxy compounds can be used to fill in small concrete sections that have settled because of poor soil preparation or frost. These formulas are also fine for filling small cracks and holes. Chipped step corners also can be fixed with this type of patch without using forms. Application should follow the manufacturer's directions.

BADLY FLAKING SURFACES

When the surface of concrete is badly flaked or pitted, it is probable that a poor job was done in the first place. It may be possible to save the old concrete without replacing it, but the repair could be only temporary, and eventually you might have to tear up the whole job. Before resorting to that drastic step, there are several things you can try.

● If only a small section is involved, scrape off all the flaking material with a wire brush. Be sure to get rid of any old concrete that has started to crack or deteriorate. Chip it out with a cold chisel and a mash hammer. Then cover the surface with vinyl or epoxy patching mix.

▲ If the deteriorated area is a large one, this method may prove too expensive, particularly since it isn't guranteed to last. One way to avoid a complete replacement is to use the old concrete as a base and pour a new surface on top of that. You must allow at least 2 inches of thickness for the new concrete. If there isn't room to pour another 2 inches on top of the old, you will have

LARGE CRACKS

Most large holes and cracks could also be filled with these modern cement patches, but the compounds are too expensive to be used on a large scale. When a lot of crack-filling is to be done, it is just as easy and considerably cheaper to use regular concrete, first undercutting the crack to a V-shape with a chisel. (Your dentist does the

Undercut crack.

Trowel in concrete.

Chip away old concrete.

Wire-brush flaking area.

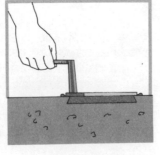

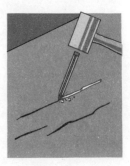

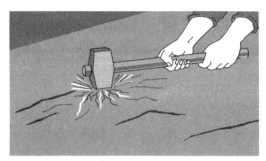

Scarify old surface by roughening it up with a sledge hammer.

to dig out 2 inches of the old concrete, in which case it is probably easier to dig up the whole thing. Most private sidewalks can be raised 2 inches without disturbing the landscape, but a driveway is another matter. Raising it that high may cause rainwater to drain into your garage, or be just enough to catch your bumper or muffler as you enter or leave. Sidewalks along the public right-of-way may be prescribed by building codes. Study the implications of a 2-inch rise in the surface before you decide to pursue that method.

Before pouring new concrete on top of the old, wire-brush the old surface and rough it up with a sledgehammer and/or an application of 20 percent muriatic acid and 80 percent water. Be sure to wear gloves and boots when working with muriatic acid, and protect your eyes. When that is done, 2-inch forms are built, as described later.

HEAVED SIDEWALK SECTIONS

● A heaved-up concrete section may be caused by severe weather contrasts or by undermining tree roots. In either case, the cure for the sorry condition involves breaking up the old slab (as far as the adjacent expansion joint) and putting in a new one. If weather conditions prevent it, or if you simply don't have the time or stomach to tackle the complete repair, it will at least

help to avoid accidents if you create a slope around the heaved portion of walk. Use the patching material discussed above to smooth around the offending section as best you can. But vow to do a complete repair job in the not-too-distant future.

▲ For the permanent repair, break up the old section using a sledgehammer or—if you can rent or borrow one—a jackhammer. Concrete was meant to last, so don't expect an easy time of it.

Once the old concrete is removed, you can determine whether or not a tree root was the cause of the problem. If so, take an axe and cut off the offending root. Any tree that is strong enough to heave concrete is strong enough to withstand the loss of one root.

If no roots are found, you can assume that Jack Frost did the dirty deed. In that case, it is wise to install wire reinforcing mesh before pouring the new section as described later in this chapter.

Temporary repair around heaved section.

Break up old section for the permanent repair.

Cut off tree roots.

Install wire mesh.

STEPS IN POURING CONCRETE

Whether you're pouring a small new section of sidewalk or a whole new driveway, the basic techniques are the same—it's merely a matter of greater or lesser effort. Just make sure that the effort is well expended and that the job is done right. Doing it right involves the following steps:

1. Preparation of the subgrade (unless you are pouring new concrete on top of old)
2. Formwork
3. Mixing
4. Placement
5. Finishing
6. Curing

Each of these steps must be done carefully and correctly. If any one of them is done improperly, the entire job will probably be ruined, and you'll be right back where you started.

SUBGRADE PREPARATION

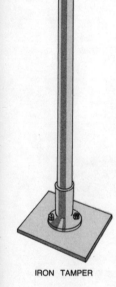

IRON TAMPER

Concrete work can be compared to baking a cake. Getting the proper ingredients together in the right proportions is most important, but you also have to find the right pan and prepare it. The "pan" in this case is the formwork. And instead of greasing the pan, you have to prepare the ground.

Second to poor mixing, the most frequent error in concrete work is poor soil preparation. Slabs will settle, crack, and fall apart in poorly prepared or compacted soil. If that was your problem before, take a good look at the subgrade. It should be free of all organic matter such as sod, grass, roots, and soft or mucky ground. If some spots are very hard and others very soft, the concrete will surely crack from settling in the softer areas. Hard spots

SELFMADE TAMPER

should be broken up, soft ones filled in and compacted.

On the other hand, do not simply remove whatever soil is under your slab and replace it with fill. If settling and cracking were not problems before, the subgrade is probably all right; as long as it is reasonably uniform and free of vegetable matter, it is better left alone. All it should need is tamping of the top portion that was disturbed by removing the old section. Undisturbed soil is better than soil that has been dug out, replaced, and poorly compacted.

If the soil is soft and highly organic, it should be dug out and replaced with fill. Remove about 4 to 6 inches of the subgrade to a depth of 8 to 10 inches below the surfaces of the adjacent sections. Be careful not to undercut the sound concrete.

Gravel, crushed stone, or blast-furnace slag can be used for fill, but sand is usually preferred for small sections because it can be leveled and compacted more easily. Rake the material, then check with a level and straightedge; it should be as level as possible. For a compactor, you can probably rent an iron tamper, or you can make your own with a 2 x 2 or 2 x 4 handle nailed to a base of ¾-inch plywood or 2 x 6 lumber. For small areas, a 2 x 4 alone will probably suffice. What you use is not as important as using it well. Make sure that you compact the soil completely. Then check it with the level, take down any high spots and fill low spots, and tamp again.

SETTING FORMS

Concrete walks and driveways are normally 4 inches thick, although you may find thinner slabs in garden walks or other walks that bear little traffic. If your driveway has any appreciable truck traffic, such as an oil delivery truck, you may want to consider a 5-inch slab. The best guideline here is to

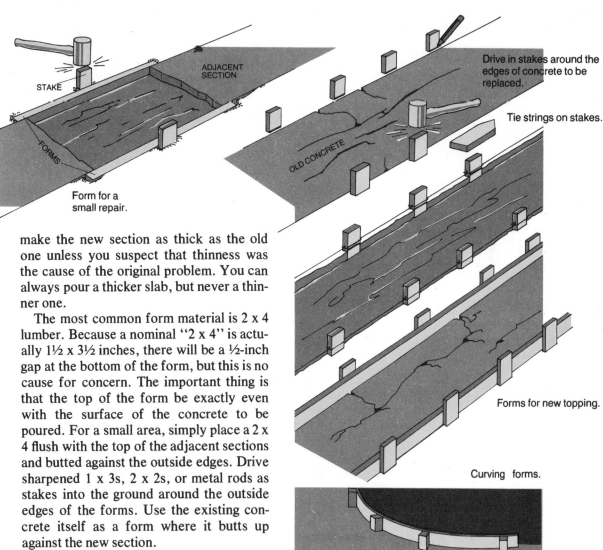

STAKE

ADJACENT SECTION

FORMS

Form for a small repair.

Drive in stakes around the edges of concrete to be replaced.

Tie strings on stakes.

OLD CONCRETE

Forms for new topping.

Curving forms.

make the new section as thick as the old one unless you suspect that thinness was the cause of the original problem. You can always pour a thicker slab, but never a thinner one.

The most common form material is 2 x 4 lumber. Because a nominal "2 x 4" is actually 1½ x 3½ inches, there will be a ½-inch gap at the bottom of the form, but this is no cause for concern. The important thing is that the top of the form be exactly even with the surface of the concrete to be poured. For a small area, simply place a 2 x 4 flush with the top of the adjacent sections and butted against the outside edges. Drive sharpened 1 x 3s, 2 x 2s, or metal rods as stakes into the ground around the outside edges of the forms. Use the existing concrete itself as a form where it butts up against the new section.

▲When replacing large pieces or an entire walk or drive, the formwork is somewhat more complicated. Assuming that the old grade was acceptable, drive in several stakes around the edges before you demolish the old work, and mark them to show the top of the walk or drive. After the old concrete has been taken out, run a string line between these marks to serve as a guide for the new forms. If there is a straight run from one section to the next, simply drive in stakes at both ends and tie the line between. Adjust the forms to that level. Line stakes should be set every 8 feet and the string pulled as taut as possible.

If the old grade wasn't correct, pour concrete to a new one. The ideal slope is ¼ inch per foot. It all depends on the terrain, though, and you can't have that type of slope on a hilly driveway. Just make sure that you don't pitch a driveway toward the garage, or a walkway toward a patio or the house. Concrete acts as a conduit for rainwater, and improper sloping is an open invitation to drainage problems.

Nail through stakes into forms.

Use double-headed nail.

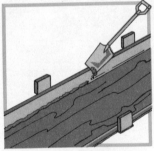

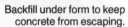

Backfill under form to keep concrete from escaping.

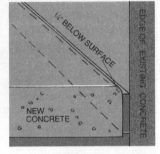

¼" BELOW SURFACE

NEW CONCRETE

EDGE OF EXISTING CONCRETE

Install isolation joints to separate floors from walls.

Use 2 x 4s for forms even though you may be pouring a 2-inch topping over old concrete. The forms must be butted firmly against the sides of the old material. Gentle curves may be formed with ¼-inch exterior plywood or one-inch lumber. Plywood, with the outside grain running vertically, or tempered hardboard are best for sharp curves.

Drive in stakes at each end of short runs and every 4 feet on long runs. Regular spacing is all right for gentle curves, but drive stakes every 1 to 2 feet for short-radius curves. For very sharp curves, you may need 2 x 4 stakes. Drive stakes tight against the outside of the forms and nail through

the stakes into the forms—hold the forms with your foot while nailing. If you have difficulty doing this, set temporary stakes on the inside of the forms to hold them during nailing, and remove them when everything is nailed together and before pouring concrete. Use double-headed nails; they are easier to pull out after the forms are removed.

▲When the stakes are all in place, backfill under the forms to keep the concrete from escaping underneath. Install isolation joints, made of ¼- or ½-inch premolded fiber (available at building supply houses), at intersections such as driveway-to-walk or walk-to-house. The joint material should be ¼ inch below the surface of the surrounding concrete.

THE PROPER MIX

Since it is vital to get the right proportions in your concrete mix, take the worry out by using premixed bags on smaller jobs. Premix saves time and trouble as well as anxiety over the right proportions. On large jobs, you can accomplish the same result by ordering "readymix" from a concrete service to be delivered by cement-mixer truck.

It is less expensive, of course, to mix your own concrete. Sometimes you may find that a concrete truck cannot get to the site, and you will have to mix your own anyway. And, unless you have several willing helpers, you will not be able to handle the large loads that readymix suppliers deliver. For one or two workers, it is easier to mix smaller loads and place them in stages.

Portland cement is purchased in bags from local building and mason supply houses. Bags weigh 94 pounds in the United States and are one cubic foot in volume. In Canada, bags weigh 80 pounds each and hold about ⅞ cubic foot.

For the average concrete application, the following proportions are ideal:

- 94 pounds of cement (one U.S. bag)
- 215 pounds of sand
- 295 pounds of coarse aggregate
- 5 gallons of water

A regular bathroom scale is accurate enough for weighing the materials. Use a 3- to 5-gallon galvanized bucket to hold the material, but be sure to weigh the pail first and deduct its weight from the weight of the material. ("Zeroing" the scale with an empty bucket may be easier on your arithmetic.) Don't put more material in the bucket than you can readily handle—it's heavy. Put the sand and aggregate into three or four buckets of equal weight. Once you get the right weight established, mark a line on the bucket for each ingredient and return the scale to the bathroom.

A simpler, although less accurate, way to measure is by volume. To achieve the ideal mix mentioned above, use 1 part portland cement to 2¼ parts sand and 3 parts aggregate. Add 5 gallons of water for each bag of cement. Both of these one-bag formulas should yield approximately ⅙ cubic yard of concrete, enough for a typical section of sidewalk.

When buying aggregates, make sure that they are clean and free of organic matter. Don't bring in stones or sand from the beach. Order fresh, clean, dry sand and gravel or crushed stone from a dealer who specializes in such materials. The coarse aggregate should be "well graded," with a range of sizes from small to large but not too many of any one size. The maximum aggregate size for a 4-inch slab should be one inch in diameter.

In most areas of the United States and all of Canada, concrete should contain an "air-entraining" agent. This can be premixed into the cement (preferably) or be added to the water. Air-entrainment causes tiny bubbles to form inside the concrete. Hardened concrete always contains some minute particles of water, and freezing temperatures cause this water to expand. This is one of the most frequent causes of concrete scaling. The microscopic bubbles created by air-entrainment act as relief valves for the expanding concrete, and also help resist the effects of salt deicers.

HOW MUCH CONCRETE?

To estimate your concrete needs, multiply length times width in feet to get the area, then multiply again by the thickness of the slab. The usual 4-inch slab is ⅓ foot thick, so take ⅓ of the area. If, for example, you are pouring a sidewalk section 4 by 4 feet, 4 inches thick, you have:

4 x 4 = 16 square feet of surface
16 x ⅓ = 5.3 cubic feet
Because there are 27 cubic feet in a cubic yard, divide your total by 27:
5.3 cubic feet ÷ 27 = .2 cubic yard

You should always figure on a little extra for waste and spillage, so ¼ cubic yard is just about right in this example. If using premix, determine the coverage on the bag (usually ⅓ cubic yard for 45 pounds, ⅔ for 90) and buy accordingly. If you are mixing your own, figure on about 1⅓ bags of portland cement, plus 1⅓ times the other ingredients used in either of the one-bag formulas previously given. (If you want to order readymix, you'll have to have a lot more concrete work to do. Most dealers require a minimum of one cubic yard per delivery.)

You may find it easier to remember that for 4-inch slabs there are 1.23 yards of concrete for every 100 square feet. For small areas, figure .12 yards for every 10 square feet. Two-inch slabs are half of that.

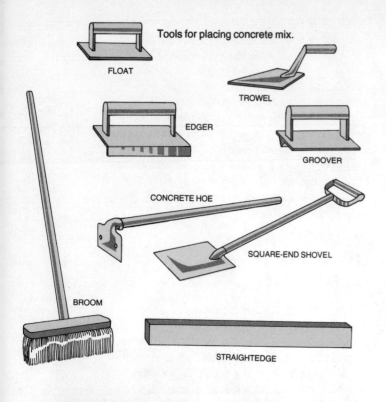

Tools for placing concrete mix.

FLOAT

TROWEL

EDGER

GROOVER

CONCRETE HOE

SQUARE-END SHOVEL

BROOM

STRAIGHTEDGE

WHEELBARROW

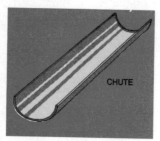

CHUTE

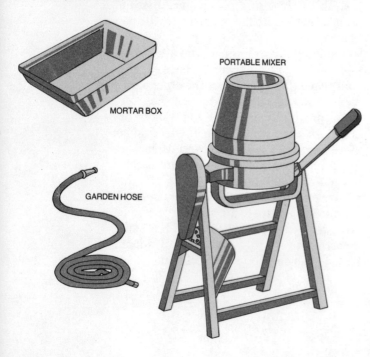

MORTAR BOX

PORTABLE MIXER

GARDEN HOSE

MIXING

Small batches of concrete can be mixed by hand on a piece of plywood. You can mix on top of existing concrete if you clean up well afterward, or in a mortar box (you may be able to rent one). For a job of any considerable size, rent a portable mixer.

Premix is dumped in a pile, then a hollow is made in the center and the label-recommended amount of water added. When mixing concrete from scratch, spread the sand out evenly on the mixing surface, then add the cement. Mix both thoroughly by turning over with a square-end shovel until they have a uniform color without streaking. Spread this mix out evenly, then add the coarse aggregate. Again turn over thoroughly. Form a hollow as with the premix.

After water has been added, use the shovel to fold all the materials over toward the center, and continue mixing until all water, cement, sand, and aggregate have been thoroughly combined.

PLACING THE MIX

When the concrete has been thoroughly mixed, or when the readymix arrives, everything should be in readiness for placing. Although job requirements may differ, most employ the following tools: concrete hoe or square-end shovel, straightedge or strike board (a straight 2 x 4 works well), float, edger, groover, trowel, broom, and garden hose. You may also need a wheelbarrow and/or chute to get the mix where you want it to go. Some sort of materials to aid the curing process should also be on hand (see CURING below). Use the hose to wet down the area before pouring concrete.

Never try to wheel concrete up a steep grade. A small grade here and there can be managed, particularly if you can get a good start. But trying to push a wheelbarrow uphill from a standing start is a heavier job than most of us can handle. If you expect difficulty in getting readymix concrete to the site, explain the problem to the dealer. He may be able to suggest a solution. If not, your only choice is machine-mixing close to the site.

Place the concrete in the forms to full depth, spading along the sides to complete filling. Try to lead the concrete as close as possible to its final position without too much dragging and shoveling. Start in one corner and continue pouring until you reach the other side. Use the shovel or concrete hoe to get as uniform coverage as possible.

When you have poured enough concrete to fill the forms, the next operations—striking off and rough-floating—should follow immediately. A prime requisite for successful finishing is that rough-floating must be completed before bleed water starts to appear on the surface of the concrete.

STRIKING OFF AND FLOATING

After placing, strike off the surface with a 2 x 4 straightedge, working it in a sawlike motion across the top of the form boards. The strike-off or "screeding" action smooths the surface while cutting off ex-

cess concrete to the proper elevation. Go over the concrete twice in this manner to take out any bumps or fill in low spots. Tilt the straightedge slightly in the direction of travel to obtain a better cutting effect.

Immediately after striking off, the surface is rough-floated to smooth it and remove irregularities. Use a wood hand float for most patchwork, but try to rent a large bull float if you are doing a big job. The float is tilted slightly away from you as you push it forward, then flattened as it is pulled back.

EDGING AND GROOVING

If you use air-entrained concrete, the finishing process can begin almost immediately after rough-floating. Even without air-entrainment, you do not have to wait long on a hot, dry, windy day. If the weather is cool and humid, however, you may be forced to wait several hours. The key to proper timing is whether or not there is water sheen on the surface. Begin when the sheen has disappeared, which happens sooner on days when quicker evaporation can be expected.

Ordinarily, the surface should be ready for finishing by the time you have finished cutting the concrete away from the forms. This is accomplished by working a pointed

Strike off the surface with a straightedge.

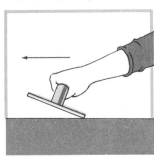
Work float forward, tilting it slightly away from you.

Flatten float if you pull it back.

Bull float.

Work trowel inside form to cut the concrete away from the form.

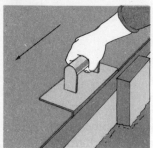

Moving edger forward.

Pulling edger back.

trowel along inside of the forms to a depth of about one inch.

The first finishing step is edging, which should take place as soon as the surface is stiff enough to hold the shape of the edging tool. Edging produces a neat, rounded corner to prevent chipping and other damage, which could be a problem once the forms are removed. The edger is run between the forms and the concrete, with the body of the tool held almost flat on the concrete surface. When moving the edger either forward or back, the leading edge should be tilted slightly upward. Be careful not to let the edger sink too deeply into the concrete, since deep indentations may be difficult to remove with subsequent finishing.

CONTROL JOINTS

A control joint is a groove cut into the concrete to keep cracks from extending throughout an entire concrete surface. In walks and drives, control joints should be spaced at intervals equal to the width of the slab. They are desirable whenever a slab extends more than 10 feet in any direction.

Most patchwork should not require new control joints. If you're replacing only a section of concrete, control joints as such will not be needed. You will recall, though, the recommendation that any bad section be replaced up to the adjacent control joints. You will have to provide new joints to replace the ones that were lost when you removed that section. And you will, of course, need new control joints if you are replacing more than one section.

Use the groover and a straightedge to make control joints. The cutting edge should be deep enough to cut into the slab about one-fourth of its thickness. In most cases, that means the cut should be about an inch deep. When replacing old control joints, place the groover bit into the wet concrete where it meets the existing work. One side of the tool body should be run

Use groover to cut a control joint into the cement.

Run groover along existing concrete edge.

Use straightedge with groover on new work.

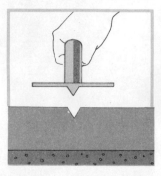

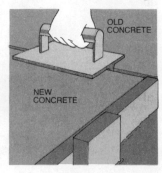

OLD CONCRETE

NEW CONCRETE

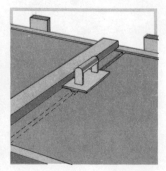

along the existing concrete while the other side runs on the new work, cutting a groove as precisely as possible between the two. Be careful not to press down too hard on the wet side so that the line goes crooked. Even pressure on the hardened side should keep the tool level.

When making control joints in completely new work, use a piece of 2 x 4 or similar board as a guide. When grooving across a sidewalk or driveway, the board should rest on, and be at right angles to, the forms. Push the groover into the concrete and move forward while applying pressure to the back of the tool. After the joint is cut, turn the tool around and pull back over the groove to provide a smooth finish.

FINISHING

After edging and grooving are completed, final floating takes place. This procedure embeds large aggregate near the surface, compacts the concrete, and removes imperfections left in the surface by previous operations. Using the wood float, work over the entire surface. Hold the float flat on the surface and use a slight sawing motion in a sweeping arc to fill in holes and smooth ridges and lumps.

Before doing anything more, compare the appearance of the finish-floated surface with that of the surrounding concrete. In many cases, this is the final step. The new surface should look slightly rough and have a nonskid texture. If it matches the old, the finishing job is done.

When the existing concrete has a glassy-smooth surface, it has no doubt been steel-troweled, and you will have to do the same to make the new surface match. Use a rectangular, steel-bladed trowel; at least two passes over the surface are necessary. If it isn't smooth enough after two, make a third. The trowel should make a ringing

Floating.

Steel-troweling.

Brooming.

Swirling.

sound as the blade passes over the hardened surface. Don't be too concerned if the new patch doesn't exactly match the old. Even an experienced mason is hard put to accomplish that.

If there are irregularly spaced scratch marks across the old surface, it was probably "broomed." To match this, go over the floated surface with a stiff-bristled "garage" broom. If the lines on the old work are wavy, swing the broom in a similar pattern. If they are straight, work the broom over the surface in straight line. Again, don't expect a perfect match. It just isn't possible.

A swirled surface is accomplished with a hand float or trowel. Try both to see which comes closer to matching the original. With either tool, work in a fanlike, semicircular motion, applying pressure as you swing your arm in an arc over the surface. Don't move your wrist, just your arm.

Cover concrete with wet burlap for curing.

Keep burlap moist, sprinkling it periodically.

Run water continuously over concrete from soaking hose.

"Ponding" to keep concrete moist for small jobs.

CURING

The chemical reaction that takes place between cement and water is called hydration, a curing process that must continue for several days to a week after placing to attain maximum durability. If too much water is lost by evaporation, the chemical reaction ceases. The same is true when temperatures get below 50 degrees F. Hydration slows almost to a standstill as the temperature approaches the freezing mark.

Curing is a vital step in concrete work. It is essential to keep water in the concrete the right length of time. As soon as the finishing process is complete and the surface is hard enough so that it will not be damaged, curing should begin. In warm weather, the curing process must continue for five days. For every 10 degrees less than 70, add an extra day (six days at 60 de-grees, seven at 50 degrees). At no time should the temperature of the concrete fall below 50 degrees. If there is a chance that this will happen, you shouldn't be laying concrete at all.

The recommended curing method for the do-it-yourselfer is to keep the concrete surface damp by covering it with wet burlap. Rinse out the burlap before use, particularly if it is new, and spread over the slab. The burlap should be checked several times a day to see that it does not dry out. Periodic sprinkling, at least daily, will keep the burlap moist.

Another method of keeping the surface wet during curing is by running a sprinkler or soaking hose continuously over the surface. Never let the surface get dry, because only partial curing will ruin the job. For small jobs, you might try "ponding"—building sand or earth dikes around the edges of the slab and filling with water. The water must be deep enough to cover the entire surface of the concrete and prevent formation of dry spots.

BLACKTOP REPAIR

The reasons for blacktop breaking up or deteriorating are similar to those for the same conditions in concrete. An additional problem with blacktop, however, is that it is easier for water, oil, etc., to get through

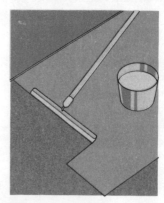
Apply sealer to blacktop.

and attack from underneath. A good sealer applied every year or two gives added protection against such damage.

Like concrete, blacktop must not be applied when the temperature is likely to fall below 50 degrees F. No matter how badly your driveway may need patching during the winter, it will just have to wait until the birds return—and probably later.

When blacktop starts to crack and break up, the deteriorated sections should be removed. Dig out the area underneath and fill in with the old broken-up blacktop. Blacktop patch is available at reasonable cost from most building supply dealers.

Tamp down the subgrade thoroughly, and fill with gravel or other solid material if the depth is more than 2 inches. Pour in the new blacktop patch and smooth over the top with a shovel. The secret of blacktop repair is that it should be tamped down thoroughly. In this case, a metal tamper is a necessity. (You should be able to rent one.) Keep tamping until the patch is smooth and level, then run over it a few times with your car's tires. Do this as gently as possible—don't skid or "burn out" or do anything else to disturb it. Your car is merely acting as a roller.

Let the patch dry and harden for a few days. It should be as good as new. Blacktop adheres well to old blacktop. You can even apply new blacktop on top of old.

1. Dig out old blacktop.

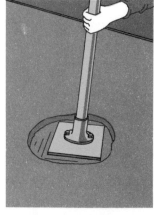

2. Tamp down subgrade.

3. Smooth patch.

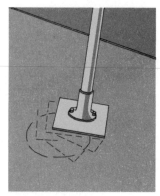

4. Tamp patch.

5. Roll patch with car.

Driveways and Sidewalks • Chapter 7

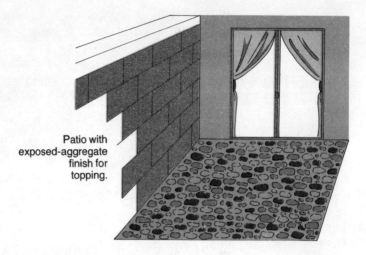

Patio with exposed-aggregate finish for topping.

8

Patio Repairs

Patios can be built of a variety of materials. The principal ones are concrete, brick, stone, and patio block, the latter being a type of flat cinder block. Although all these materials are long-lasting when used correctly, they are subject to the same types of stresses as are driveways and sidewalks. There is also the frequent problem of poor original construction.

 ## CONCRETE PATIO REPAIRS

Since a concrete patio is simply a concrete slab, just like a driveway or sidewalk, repair techniques are the same as those detailed in the preceding chapter. Use vinyl latex or epoxy patching mixes for small holes and cracks or wherever feathered edges are needed. For large cracks and holes, undercut the damaged portion and fill with standard concrete mix. Replace badly damaged sections by digging out the old work and forming, etc., as directed in CHAPTER 7.

When the entire surface needs repair, patios are much better suited to the addition of a 2-inch topping course than walks or driveways, since the additional height usually causes no problems. There should be no difficulty with people tripping over raised areas, as there might be on a side-walk, and you don't have to worry about damaged mufflers or drainage problems, as you would for a driveway. Attached patios are ordinarily sloped away from the house and toward the lawn, where rainwater will do more good than harm.

Raising the patio height may even be beneficial. Many patios are situated below the first-floor level of the house, and often the step down is too high to begin with. But raising the patio could pose problems if the house is laid on a slab and the patio is almost at first-floor level already.

If you are considering topping the patio, an excellent and attractive way to do this is with exposed-aggregate concrete. (Exposed aggregate is often referred to as terrazzo, but true terrazzo utilizes a different installation technique and contains decorative and more expensive aggregates such as quartz, granite, or marble chips.) In an exposed-aggregate finish, the aggregates in the mix are kept near the surface, and the cement paste that usually covers them is washed and brushed away. Although regular aggregates can be used, the surface is much more colorful and handsome if rounded, beach-type stones are used. An "ex-ag" surface is highly durable and slip-resistant as well as attractive.

When building a new exposed-aggregate concrete slab, many contractors do the job in two stages—a base course topped with the ex-ag course. Topping an existing patio with a layer of exposed-aggregate concrete follows the same principle.

To lay a 2-inch topping course, order or mix concrete with a low "slump" (a measure of workability). There should be a high proportion of coarse-to-fine aggregates so that the larger ones stay near the surface. With only 2 inches of concrete to lay, it is easier to keep the larger aggregates near the top than if you were starting from scratch.

The usual concrete construction techniques can be followed, except that rough-floating is done gently to keep the larger stones from being pressed down too far. When the water sheen disappears, and the concrete can bear a man's weight on a piece of one-inch lumber without indentation, it's time to expose the aggregate. Begin washing and brooming as described below, but if

the stones become dislodged or overexposed, wait another 15 to 30 minutes, then try again.

Two persons are better than one for this operation. One worker washes down the surface with a fine spray from a garden hose while the other brushes the surface lightly with a stiff-bristled broom, preferably nylon. If you can't find a helper, alternately wash and broom. The combination of washing and brooming should remove all the cement paste and film from the surface of the aggregate.

Be prepared for some hard brushing, because any cement paste remaining on the surface will leave it looking dull and lifeless. A special ex-ag broom, which is attached to the hose and sprays water at the same time, is ideal for this job if you can borrow or rent one. If, in spite of your efforts, the surface looks rather grimy, give it another rubdown with a 20 percent muriatic acid solution. Follow the usual precautions when working with the acid—wear protective clothing and protect your eyes.

"Seeding" is another method by which the do-it-yourselfer can achieve an ex-

Scrub with muriatic acid solution, if brushing did not help.

Kneel on board to test hardness of concrete.

Wet and brush the surface (try to get a helper).

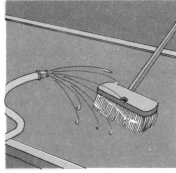

Ex-ag broom.

posed-aggregate finish. The topping mix is spread in the usual manner, but is leveled off ⅜ inch to ½ inch below the top of the forms. This allows room for the aggregate to be spread over the top of the concrete. The base coat is struck off and floated as usual. The aggregate stone is then spread evenly over the surface with a shovel and filled in by hand where necessary until the entire surface is covered completely with aggregate. If the first few stones start to sink to the bottom, wait another 30 minutes or so until the mix is a little stiffer.

When there is an even stone cover, tap the aggregate down into the still pliable concrete with a 2 x 4 or a wood float. Then go over the entire surface with the float, working the stones well into the mix until they are completely covered by cement paste. The surface will then look just about as it did before you started seeding.

 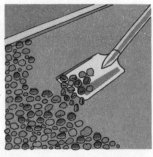

1. Level topping mix off below forms.
2. Spread aggregate stone evenly over the surface.

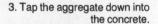

3. Tap the aggregate down into the concrete.
4. Go over the entire surface with the float.

Wait about another hour, until the seeded slab can bear the weight of a man on a piece of lumber. Washing and brooming can then proceed as above.

BRICK PATIOS

Brick patios are normally built by one of two methods. The easiest both to lay and repair is the brick-in-sand patio, in which a bed of sand is put down and leveled. Sometimes cement is mixed with the base sand for a more stable bed. Then the bricks are simply set on top, with more sand being swept in later to fill the joints. Brick patios may also be put down over a mortar bed, with mortar joints between the bricks.

Although a brick-in-sand patio is more likely to heave and settle than the other type, especially over the winter months, it is simpler to repair. Any bricks that come up or sink down below the level of the others are removed. You may need an old screwdriver or other tool to dislodge the first, but the adjacent ones can be lifted out easily by hand.

If the bricks in question have settled, lay in some extra sand (any sand will do for this—even beach sand) and tamp it down well. Watering helps to settle the sand and compact it. When the bed is satisfactory, reinstall the bricks the same way they were laid before. In this type of patio, the bricks are butted as tightly as possible against one another. When all have been replaced, spread more sand over the top and work it down between the cracks with a stiff-bristled broom. Spray the patio with a hose, then sweep in more sand. It may take three or more similar applications before the brick is again locked into position so that no more sand can be worked in.

Since mortared brick patios should be set on top of a concrete base slab, heaving and settling of the brick itself should be rela-

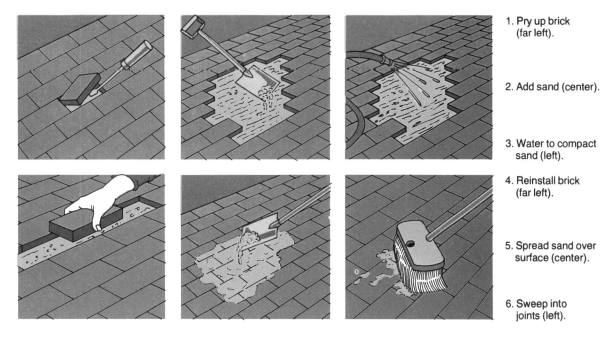

1. Pry up brick (far left).

2. Add sand (center).

3. Water to compact sand (left).

4. Reinstall brick (far left).

5. Spread sand over surface (center).

6. Sweep into joints (left).

tively rare. If a few bricks do exhibit such problems, remove them by chipping out the mortar with a brick chisel or cold chisel. You probably won't be able to remove all the mortar, but you should get enough so that you can pry up the bricks with a chisel or wrecking bar.

If the problem is settling, chip out any crumbly mortar underneath and replace with new. Lay in enough new mortar to bring the surface level with the rest. Standard or common brick is nominally 2¾ inches in depth, counting mortar, with the actual brick size 2¼ inches. But not all brick is alike, so measure what you have.

For mortar, it is easiest to purchase premixed mortar from a masonry or building supply dealer. If you mix your own, use the same proportions used for laying a new bed (see below).

▲When the brick is heaved, it is more difficult to repair. The brick and mortar must be removed and the concrete base chipped off to bring it down to the surrounding level. Then proceed as above. If tree roots have caused the heaving, remove all the concrete in the affected section, chop off the root as far back as possible, then pour new concrete. After curing, replace the brick as above.

Chip out mortar (far left).

Pry up brick (center).

Lay in new mortar (left).

When the patio is badly heaved or settled, it is probable that the concrete was poorly laid originally. In that case, all the brick will have to be removed, the concrete broken up or topped, and a whole new patio installed. Lay the slab as directed in CHAPTER 7. After thorough curing, make a mortar of 1 part masonry cement (premixed with lime) and 4½ parts of sand. Add water, a little at a time, until the mix has the consistency of soft mud. Spread a ½-inch bed over a small section at a time. After removing as much old mortar as possible from the old brick (or using new brick), "butter" the brick on both edges and one end with ½ inch of mortar and lay into the mortar bed. Continue working in this manner a section at a time until the repair is completed.

Spread mortar.

Lay brick into mortar bed.

"Butter" brick.

Force mortar into joint.

Fortunately, most repair jobs to mortared brick involve only repointing or tuck-pointing crumbling mortar. Since you won't want to repeat the job in the too-near future, all weak or loose joints should be repointed along with the ones that are obviously crumbled.

●The crumbled mortar should be chiseled out to a depth of about an inch, even though the deterioration is only at the surface. The greater depth will give the mortar a better hold. Wear safety glasses or goggles when doing this type of work to prevent eye injuries from flying mortar chips.

The mortar mix used for tuck-pointing should be stiffer than normal mixes. One part masonry cement is mixed with 2¼ to 3 parts of clean sand, with less water than for normal use. The mix is about right when it slides from the trowel in a sideways position, but clings when the trowel is turned upside down. Special repointing mortar can be bought at most building supply dealers.

After dampening all the areas to be repointed, force the mortar into the joint with a trowel. Do the short joints first, then the long ones.

FLAGSTONE PATIO REPAIRS

The problems encountered with flagstone are very similar to those with brick patios. Most stone patios are laid in mortar, but plain sand is often used. Use the same repair procedures for stone as you would use for brick laid in the same way.

One difficulty may be in removing large stones. They are quite heavy, and you may need either a helper or some device to remove stones. One way to remove them without help is by placing a piece of pipe or a wood dowel or steel rod next to the stone to be removed, and lifting the stone just enough to rest a corner on the rod. A pry

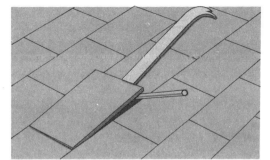

Lift at least a corner of the stone onto the rod (right).

Roll the stone out of the way (far right).

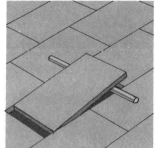

bar can help you accomplish this. The stone can then be shoved onto the rod and rolled over out of the way so that you can work beneath.

If stone has been broken badly, it may need replacement. With random shaped and colored stone, you should be able to find a replacement easily enough. The stone doesn't have to match its mates in either size or shape, although it should vaguely resemble the others. Try to select a piece that is shaped similarly to the one being replaced. It can be somewhat smaller, but not bigger. Fill in the surrounding spaces with mortar.

You'll have a tougher time finding a replacement when your patio is the more formal type, with matched rectangular stones. Color is usually not a problem, because few are exactly alike anyway, but you will have to find a piece that matches the damaged one in size. If you can't find one, have the stone dealer cut one to your specifications.

Try to avoid having to cut stone to fit. It *can* be cut with a cold chisel and a heavy mash hammer, but that is at best an inexact science. If you must do it, score a line first on all sides with a chisel, then keep banging at it on one side and then the other until it breaks. Unfortunately, it often breaks in the wrong place, so buy a couple of pieces.

Cutting stone with a cold chisel.

Since stone comes in various thicknesses, be sure to get one that is the same as the one it is replacing—or as close as possible. If you have to choose between a slightly thicker or thinner one, choose the thinner and fill the gap with new mortar.

PATIO BLOCK

Patio block is made in standard sizes. Damaged blocks are fairly simple to replace. Procedures are the same as for brick. You shouldn't have to do any cutting; but if you do, it's easy to cut with a brick chisel and a heavy hammer.

9

Pool Care

T HE SWIMMING POOL used to be the super symbol of Hollywood success, but today you can find swimming pools in the most humble urban and suburban backyards. New methods and new materials, along with new affluence, account for this pool proliferation. Crowded public beaches accessible only by crowded highways are the determining factors that cause many families to provide their own facilities for "getting in the swim."

To insure season-long swimming fun, a certain amount of time has to be devoted to the "non-fun" aspects of swimming pools—the care and maintenance of the pool. Basically, it is a simple job if done properly and at the required intervals. When these routine tasks are neglected, trouble begins.

POOL CHEMICALS

One of the most important aspects of pool care is maintaining a proper chemical balance of the water. A glass of water coming out of the tap looks and (usually) tastes clean and clear. Put the same water in a 20 x 40-foot pool and it may look entirely different (taste is quite another matter).

That's why you shouldn't use your pool the first day you fill it up, regardless of how tempting it is and how hot the weather. The first thing you should do is turn on the filter and let it run for a day. The filter will remove the minerals and other solids that are present in most water. Any turbidity in the water should be removed, and the water should look sparkling clear after the first day.

From the very first day you fill your pool, its purity must be guarded by a chemical disinfectant. Some purifying agent, whether it be chlorine, bromine, or iodine, must be maintained in the pool water; and enough of it must remain in the water to kill disease-carrying bacteria that are brought into the water by bathers.

Chlorine is the most widely used disinfectant. Ideally it should be used at one part per million (ppm), and must have at least 0.6 ppm of "free residual chlorine." The actual ratio is really very small, since 100 percent activity is gained by only one drop of chlorine for every one million drops of water.

ROUTINE CLEANING

In addition to keeping the proper chemical balance, a few other things should be done to keep your pool clean and fresh.

Manually skimming the pool's surface is one. You'll need a standard "leaf skim-

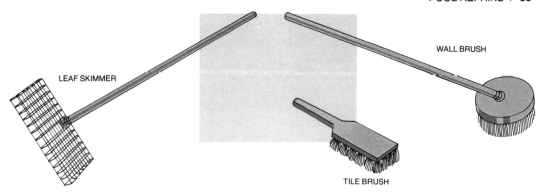

LEAF SKIMMER

WALL BRUSH

TILE BRUSH

mer," a netlike pool-cleaning tool designed especially to rid the pool's surface of leaves, bugs, debris, and other floating contaminants. Most leaf skimmers are equipped with long handles to enable you to reach the pool's center while standing on the deck.

You should also brush down walls and tile regularly. You'll need a stiff-bristled tile brush to clean near the waterline and a wall brush to clean the walls below.

Vacuuming the pool bottom is yet another chore. You'll need a special pool vacuum for this. There are many models and types. Consult your dealer as to the types best suited to your pool.

Don't forget to clean the built-in skimmer's basket and the hair-line strainer in the pump. No special equipment is needed for this. Remove the skimmer basket and the hair-line strainer from the pump. Dispose of the debris that has collected in them and replace them. This should be done as frequently as possible; daily is preferred, or even more often during the spring and fall when there is a heavy fall-out of flower petals or leaves from trees and bushes. Failure to keep the strainer clean will result in reduced circulation of the water through the pump and filter.

Clean the filter regularly. A dirty filter will result in decreased recirculation and consequent dirty water. Consult the directions of the filter manufacturer for the cor-rect procedure for your particular filter. Most likely you should "backwash," or reverse the flow of water.

Hose the deck clean. A garden hose is all you need. This should be done during every pool-cleaning.

POOL REPAIRS

A properly designed and installed swimming pool should last many years before repairs are required, provided that normal maintenance routine is faithfully followed. Major cracks or breaks in a concrete or Gunite pool are best repaired by a professional. Minor cracks and holes can easily be filled by the do-it-yourselfer.

The pool must be drained at least below the level of the damaged area. Chip away all loose concrete from the crack and wire-brush the area clean (see CHAPTER 7). Butyl

Remove and clean skimmer basket.

rubber is the most easily applied material for such repairs—look for it at your hardware store in both paste and liquid form. Work the paste into the crack or hole with a putty knife, smoothing it with the surface. A waterproof liquid rubber is then applied

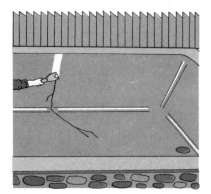

Work rubber paste into crack.

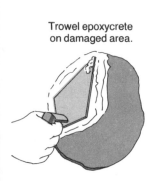

Trowel epoxycrete on damaged area.

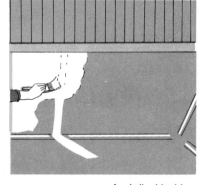

Apply liquid rubber over entire surface.

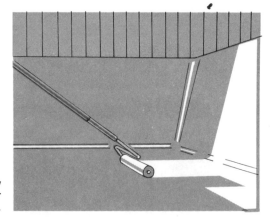

Apply all-weather sealer.

over the entire surface with a brush, roller, or spray gun. The liquid immediately forms a seamless membrane that protects the patch. It should be allowed to set for 12 to 18 hours (check label directions) and will bond perfectly to the concrete.

For larger holes and crevices, a special epoxy (again, see your hardware dealer or a swimming pool supplier) can be mixed with cement to form an impregnable, waterproof "epoxycrete." This is then troweled onto the damaged area, forming a smooth barrier to protect the surface.

As a preventive measure, you can apply an all-weather sealer to the pool walls. This will prevent cracking, powdering, chipping, or staining of the concrete caused by freezing or most chemicals. It is applied with a roller, mop, or brush at any temperature above 40 degrees. It dries to a glossy finish.

Accidental rips or cuts in a vinyl pool liner can be repaired with a special kit available at most hardware stores and pool supply dealers. Follow the manufacturer's directions.

PAINTING

Many concrete pool owners leave their pools unpainted, but paint does make a pool more attractive. The trouble with painting is that it's like the first drink for an alcoholic. You'll have to keep up the paint job once it's applied, and repainting will be necessary every few years.

There are two main points regarding pool painting. First, use alkali-resistant paints for concrete or Gunite. Second, make sure that the surface is prepared properly.

● Remove the water and repair all cracked or damaged areas to present a smooth surface throughout (same techniques as described in CHAPTER 7). If the paint is just dull or rubbed off, a thorough scrubbing is all that is necessary. If there is peeling or

Plug all openings with rubber plugs.

Stuff semi-inflated tube into skimmer.

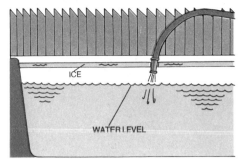

Check water level below ice and refill if it has receded.

flaking, it may be necessary to remove the old paint completely. If so, sandblasting is the best way. You can rent the equipment, but it is probably best to have professional sandblasters do the job.

WINTERIZING

In most parts of North America, there are at least a few months of the year when the weather is too cold for swimming. It is most important to leave the water in a pool. The water inside the pool serves to brace the walls against pressures created by frozen or shifting earth on the outside walls.

Before shutting your pool down for the winter clean it thoroughly. Lower the water to below the inlet suction fitting. Remove the lights, and drain all lines at lowest points. Insert rubber plugs tightly in all openings so that no water may enter.

Fill the pool again to within two inches of the bottom of the skimmer opening. Make certain that the main drain valve is closed off. Add an extra-heavy dose of chlorine. Spread the pool cover if you are using one.

Place all removed parts in a dry, warm place and properly oil, grease, or paint where necessary. Plug all lines so that vermin or mice cannot enter the system. Remove the diving board and store it on its edge. Disconnect all electrical energy. Stuff a semi-inflated bicycle tube into the skimmer to absorb pressures created by freezing and thawing.

Check the pool from time to time. If water has receded below the ice on top, refill with a garden hose until the water meets the ice. Suspended ice can cause pool damage.

POOL "FEEDING"

To keep you and your family "in the swim" throughout the season, these simple rules are suggested by the National Swimming Pool Institute:

Don't be a know-it-all. Read carefully the directions for all chemicals you intend to add.

Don't overdose. Measure exact amounts. Pool chemicals—like medicine—should be used only in specified amounts. Too much can cause irritating side-effects.

Don't guess. Take time to learn to use a test kit. Be sure to replace reagents (test fluids) each season to assure accuracy.

Establish a routine for testing and treatment. A few minutes every day— or every other day—can make the job easy and assure you a pool in tiptop shape.

Don't work too hard. If you find that taking care of your pool is too much work, check yourself—you are doing something wrong.

10

Storm!

EVEN THE WEATHER forecasters have trouble predicting what will happen in a storm, so what is a poor homeowner to do? One thing he can do is to be prepared, and be aware that just about anything might happen. Forewarned is forearmed—or at least armed enough to have a fighting chance when the wind starts to howl and the snow starts to pile up.

THE EMERGENCY TOOL KIT

Undoubtedly, you keep your toolbox neatly packed and out of the way in your home workshop. But when a storm threatens, you should make up an emergency toolbox, with various tools and materials that might come in handy if an emergency arises. You should include a claw hammer and an assortment of nails, a screwdriver, pliers, and a knife. A staple gun with a good supply of staples should also be there. At least one flashlight is a must—and make sure the batteries are in good working condition. A couple of kerosene lanterns can be most helpful. A supply of candles should also be kept nearby, along with something to hold them, even if it's your collection of old Chianti bottles.

Keep a loaded calking gun nearby. A can of asphalt cement should also be in your arsenal. A couple of large sheets of poly-ethylene (available at any hardware store) can prove invaluable. Wire and rope and several lengths of 1 x 2 or 1 x 3 lumber are other items that may come in handy, as will a roll of masking tape. Rock salt and electric heating cable provide two different methods of attacking ice buildup.

Think about the worst that might happen during a storm and try to visualize how you might cope with it. This will give a clue as to what you should have on hand. You can hope that you never have to use all these items, but the small expenditure required to be prepared is worth the peace of mind.

WINDOW BREAKAGE

When a falling tree branch smashes through a window, you probably don't want to take the time to reglaze it, and in fact it may be impossible to do so with Jack Frost nipping at your fingers. This is one place where your polyethylene sheeting will do the job—if not as well as the glass, at least enough to keep out the wind and the snow. Staple the sheeting around the window frame, doubling it at the edges for additional strength. To seal the edges, use masking tape.

If you weren't foresighted enough to lay in a supply of polyethylene, you can, of course, use other materials to cover the opening. A piece of corrugated cardboard cut to the proper dimensions and stapled or taped in place will do the job—at least until it becomes saturated with water, when you can replace it with another piece of cardboard. Even a blanket tacked over the opening is better than nothing at all, although it will shut out the light, and you may never even know when the storm has subsided.

ROOF LEAKS

When your roof springs a leak during a storm, it would be the height of idiocy to attempt a repair from the outside. Just do what you can from underneath, as outlined in CHAPTER 2. After the storm, it may be possible to make a temporary repair from above if the leak is close enough to the edge of the roof that you can reach it from a ladder. Do not attempt to go on the roof whenever it is wet or covered with snow or ice. Use the plastic sheeting for temporary repair. Slip the plastic under the course of shingles above the leaking area, which you can mark by inserting a piece of wire through the leak from underneath. Staple the sheeting to the roof, then calk around the edges. If the wind is blowing and threatens to lift up the patch, nail 1 x 2 strips around the exposed edges. When you later make a permanent repair the nail holes will have to be filled, but it's certainly better than having water pour through the leak.

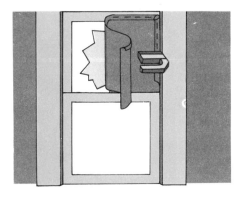

Staple sheeting over broken window.

Leakage may be caused when water from thawing snow on the roof can't run off because the gutters are frozen. The water backs up under the roof shingles and finds its way inside the house, usually causing extensive damage. You can prevent this type of damage by making sure that gutters and downspouts are kept clear so that water can flow off freely. An electric heating cable may be run along the lower edge of the roof above the gutters (see CHAPTER 2); it should be turned on during a storm before snow can accumulate.

Temporary roof repair: Staple sheeting over leak (right).

Calk around edges (below left).

Nail board around edges (below right).

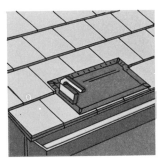

ICY WALKS

It is elementary to keep sidewalks free of ice. An icy sidewalk is an invitation to injuries and lawsuits. Chemical melters such as rock salt will do the job, although they may cause some damage to concrete as well as corrosion to cars that are driven over them. These consequences are certainly small compared to the alternatives. You might also consider keeping a large supply of clean sand, and use it to skidproof walks and driveways. It is easy to sweep away when there is no longer a need for it.

FALLEN POWER LINES

When a tree limb comes crashing down in front of your house carrying a live power line with it, you've got a real problem. Get on the phone and report it immediately to the power company. This may take some doing, because people all over the area with similar problems will also be trying to reach the power company; but keep trying. This is a necessary first step.

Post large signs on both sides of the live wire, warning passersby:

"DANGER!
FALLEN POWER LINE!
KEEP AWAY!"

Stake these to the ground or otherwise fasten them securely and far enough away from the wire so that there is no danger. If it is dark, place kerosene lanterns near the downed line. Flares are also good for this purpose, but they must be replaced periodically. Keep the warnings posted and the lanterns or flares burning until the utility company arrives. Never attempt to move branches or other debris from the power line, or anywhere even close to it.

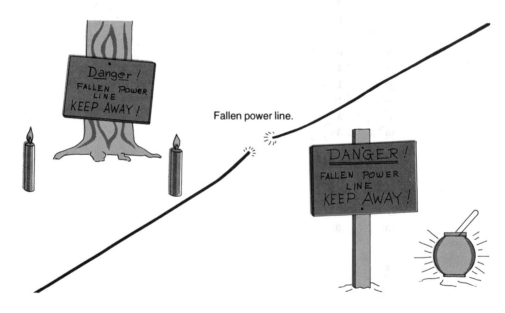

Fallen power line.

11

If You're Buying . . .

WHEN YOU'RE buying a new home, there are many things to consider. Obviously, very important considerations are the quality of construction and the condition of the house. If it's a brand-new home, you will want to go over the specifications and make sure that all the materials are of the best quality you can afford. When the house is being built for you, one concern is the workmanship. The model always looks good, but will they build yours the same way? And will all the specifications be followed? These questions are impossible to answer when you sign on the dotted line. You simply have to trust the builder, which is worrisome. During construction, you should make frequent inspections, just to make sure your trust was well placed.

When you buy an existing home, the problems are different. The guesswork is gone—the house is there for you to examine. The workmanship is obvious in most cases. The materials are often hidden, and you have no specifications to rely on. How thick, for example, is the insulation? You can usually look at attic insulation (but not always). There is no way of determining what's behind the walls.

You will be able to determine an existing home's general condition, as well as getting a good idea of workmanship and materials, by a thorough inspection. This doesn't mean that you can anticipate every problem that may turn up if you buy, but a good inspection should give you enough information so that you can determine what shape the house is in and what major problems you can expect to encounter.

STARTING YOUR INSPECTION TOUR

A routine inspection begins at the bottom. Unless the home is built on a slab, the foundation should extend at least 6 inches above the finished ground level. Be on the lookout for large vertical cracks, which can mean that the house has settled considerably. Hairline cracks in concrete are almost always present because of the nature of the material; these are no cause for alarm. Watch out, though, for uneven or honeycombed concrete or crumbling, broken corners. These are signs of poor workmanship and could mean future—and major—problems and expenses.

If the foundation or walls are of masonry, check the joints carefully. Pick at some of the mortar with a pocketknife to see if it crumbles easily (but you'd better okay this with the homeowner first). When in doubt, ask the owner if you can drive a nail into the mortar. If the mortar is skimpy, the nail will not hold.

Also check above the foundation for the existence of metal termite shields if that is a problem in your area. Termites can undermine the house if left unchecked, although this fear is often exploited out of context by avaricious termite-inspection firms. Do look for muddy tunnels on the concrete foundation, or traces of sawdust where no sawing was done. Dig your penknife into a joist or beam to see if it encounters resistance. If it doesn't and the wood is soft or decayed inside, it is a sign of some kind of problem—possibly serious. Carpenter ants or dry rot could be the cause as well as termites, but it's trouble in any case.

If the house is built over a crawl space, look inside and check the girders and joists for signs of decay. Observe the framing and subfloor for moisture stains. Excessive dampness in the crawl space could indicate a serious problem.

The house should be on a higher eleva-

To assure drainage away from the house, it should be built on a higher elevation than the surrounding land.

tion than the surrounding land, if only slightly, to insure proper drainage. The slope from the foundation or slab should be at least ½ inch per foot, but you don't have to measure it. You can usually "eyeball" the grade to determine whether there will proper rain runoff. Also make sure that all gutters and downspouts drain either into a storm sewer or onto splash blocks and from there harmlessly onto the grass away from the house.

Before you leave the foundation area, check the basement windows. Do they fit snugly against the foundation walls? Are there adequate and free-draining wells around each one to prevent runoff into the basement?

While your mind is still attuned to concrete and masonry, look at the sidewalks and driveways. Are the surfaces level and free of flaking, large cracks, or other deterioration? Are bricks, stones, etc., well mortared, or is the mortar in need of repointing? Do driveways drain away from the garage, and walkways away from the house or flower beds? See CHAPTER 7 to determine what repairs are needed. Some are simple, some quite extensive (and expensive).

ABOVE THE FOUNDATION

Before you begin a more detailed inspection of your prospective new home, give it a "once over lightly." Silly as it may sound, see if the walls look plumb and the corners square. You don't expect a house to be so poorly built that it has a noticeable tilt, but it can and does happen. Is there a sag in the roof? It's doubtful that such major defects can exist very long without the place collapsing, but it is a possibility. Make sure.

Now go up close and examine the siding materials. For painted wood, see if the

SHOULD YOU STILL BUY? / 93

paint film is dense or opaque, or if the wood is showing through. Is the paint blistering, chalking, or alligatoring (see CHAPTER 4)? This can be repaired, of course, but an exterior paint job will cost money—and time, if you do it yourself. Check out the wood. Lap siding should be nailed evenly, with sufficient overlap and tight butt joints. Corners should be mitered or butted snugly against vertical corner boards. Shingles should have plenty of overlap. The wood should not be deteriorated.

Brick or stone veneer should be well mortared. Use the knife or nail test mentioned above. Look for rust stains on masonry or wood, a sign of cheap hardware or the wrong kind of nails. Look at the calking around doors, windows, chimneys, etc. Is it crumbling? Check the protective flashing around these openings. It should be made of noncorrosive metal. Is there proper weatherstripping? Are the sills pitched away from the house for proper drainage?

Although you may not want to go up on the roof at this time for inspection, look at downspouts and gutters. Are there obvious rust spots or debris accumulations in the gutters? These, too, can be repaired, as in CHAPTER 2, but it means more time and money. Can you see any loose roof shingles from the ground? If so, there may be a lot more trouble when you look closely.

If there are porches, see if they sag. Are there loose steps, uneven floors, deteriorated railings and floorboards? Is there a good cover of deck paint on the flooring? Again, all is fixable (see CHAPTER 6), but it's more money to be laid out, and it gives you a clue to the attitude of the seller of the house.

Is there a swimming pool? If there is an above-ground pool, do the owners plan on taking it along? If so, there will be lots of grass for you to plant, probably some grading, and maybe some landfill. A built-in pool will stay with the house, of course. Do you want it? Is the concrete in good shape,

or the vinyl liner? How about the maintenance equipment, the heater, etc. Fix-ups are discussed in CHAPTER 9, but deduct the cost from your offer.

UP ON THE ROOF

Your preliminary inspection ordinarily does not include a trip to the roof, but be sure to go up there before you put any money on the line. Take a good look, too, because roof repairs can be very costly, and a poor roof can cause lots of troubles underneath.

Check for loose shingles. If there is general deterioration, a new roof may be in order. Look carefully at the hip joints and valleys, and especially the flashing around chimneys, dormers, or valleys. Does the flashing need calking or replacement? Check the condition of chimney mortar while you're up there.

Before you descend, take a closer look at the gutters and downspouts. Are they sagging or rotted? Are there accumulations of leaves and debris in the downspouts? See CHAPTER 2 for an idea of what you're in for if repairs to roof or gutters are in order.

SHOULD YOU STILL BUY?

The fact that something is wrong with the house doesn't necessarily mean that you shouldn't buy it. There will always be a certain amount of maintenance, and just as surely there will always be some neglect, especially in an older home. Unless you suspect structural damage, the best course is to estimate the cost of repairs if done by professionals (even though you may do them yourself), and deduct that from what you intend to pay for the house. This doesn't mean that you necessarily value the

If You're Buying . . . ● Chapter 11

house at, say, $40,000, and refuse to pay more than $35,000 because you estimate repairs at $5,000—particularly if the owner is asking $50,000. Home buying is a give-and-take proposition, and the true value is what you and the seller reluctantly finally agree on. But if you have a thorough list of defects and reliable estimates, you have a bargaining tool.

PROFESSIONAL INSPECTION SERVICES

For a fee of from $50 to $150, depending on the area and whether the inspectors are professional engineers or appraisers, you can obtain a professional consultation on the condition of your prospective home. Obviously, you can't call in an inspector every time you think you *might* want to buy a house, but if you've narrowed your choice down to one and you're very serious about buying, this service may be well worth your while.

The professional consultation can not only be a worthwhile investment for your own peace of mind, but it can also be a valuable negotiating tool. No matter how careful you are in your own inspection tour, you may miss structural flaws that only an expert can determine. The expert may also resolve any doubts you might have as to roof condition, foundation defects, etc. This is recommended particularly if the home is very old or very new. A very old home may have outlived its usefulness; a new one might not yet have exhibited the signs of decay that could already be there. Homes that have been up a few years have usually gone through the break-in period and should not yet be approaching the problems of old age.

No matter who does the inspecting, you or a professional (friends are unreliable and may look for flaws just to show you how smart they are), just make sure that it is done. Knowing *before* buying is much more satisfactory than finding out afterwards. At least you know what the problems are. It's not knowing (and probably paying too much) that hurts.

Index